W9-AXX-649

Under The Mohegan Sun

Mohegan

A Celebration of Cuisine & Culture

Under The Mohegan Sun

Published by
Mohegan Tribal Gaming Authority

1 Mohegan Sun Boulevard
Uncasville, Connecticut 06382
860-862-8000

Executive Editor: Gary Crowder
Executive Chef: Michael Luboff
Project Manager: Carroll Collins
Photographic images for the endsheets, cover insert,
pages 2, 11, 25, 35, 79 and 139: ©Ellen Hoverkamp
Food Photography: ©Chris Vaccaro
Food Stylist: Cindy Salvato
Photograph on page 7: ©Mark Brett
Other photography: Mohegan Sun historical archives

ISBN: 0-9760502-0-X
Library of Congress Number: 2004114724

Edited, Designed, and Manufactured by Favorite Recipes® Press
an imprint of

FRP

P.O. Box 305142
Nashville, Tennessee 37230
800-358-0560

Art Director: Steve Newman
Designers: Brad Whitfield and Susan Breining
Editorial Project Manager: Jane Hinshaw
Managing Editor: Mary Cummings
Operations Director: Ed Arndt
Publishing Consultant: Dee Plunkett

Manufactured in the United States of America
First Printing 2005
15,000 copies

Preface

The recipes served in the restaurants at Mohegan Sun and brought to you in this book contain the ingredients that have sustained the Mohegan Tribe for centuries. They also represent the passion and dedication of our culinary team. Here under the roof of the Mohegan Sun you will find a diverse and exceptional array of dining and entertainment options. This book, *Under the Mohegan Sun,* was designed to share our culinary culture and passion with you, in the sincere hope that you will find spiritual and nutritional sustenance.

Weegwasun, May You Live Happily,

GARY S. CROWDER
Senior Vice President Food and Beverage

Assistant Executive Chefs-Richard Doucette and Guy Fodor
Executive Pastry Chef-Lynn Mansel
Executive Sous Chefs-Chip Miller, Craig Schmalz, Paul van der Putten, Marshall Lewis, and Jeff Gordon
Quality Assurance Chef-Carolyn Dziengiel
*Executive Sous Chef Craig Schmalz-*TRIBAL SOUPS & CHOWDERS
*Chef Dave Marchand-*FIDELIA'S
*Chef Rob Sargent-*MOHEGAN TERRITORY
*Chef Matt Sadowski-*CHIEF'S DELI
*Chef Paul Zenga-*THE COVE
*Chef John Nordin-*RAIN
*Chef Jeffrey Steelman-*TODD ENGLISH'S TUSCANY
*Chef Napoleon Hidalgo-*POMPEII & CAESAR
*Chef John Lee-*BAMBOO FOREST
*Chef Aiman Saad-*THE LONGHOUSE
*Executive Pastry Chef Lynn Mansel-*DESSERTS

Acknowledgements

To create a delicious recipe, the finest ingredients are blended together in just the right mix to maximize flavor and presentation.

To create this cookbook, the talents of a great team of people were blended together to deliver a book that combines Mohegan Sun cuisine and culture. My sincere thanks to each of you who were involved in the project.

- To the Mohegan Tribal Nation for their approval, support, and historical perspective. Special thanks to *Bruce "Two Dogs" Bozsum, Faith Damon Davison, Sister Bette-Jean,* and *Suzette Tanguay.*

- To *Dr. Jeffrey Bendremer* for the Indian artifacts supplied for photography courtesy of the Mohegan Tribe Historic Preservation Department.

- To *Captain Phil Russell, Mike Russell, Timothy Rollins,* and *Barbara Breece* at the Mohegan Aquaculture Center for treating us to a day of oyster fishing at beautiful Stonington Harbor.

- To *George Galinsky,* Vice President, Advertising and Public Relations, *Jason Pedley,* Copywriter/Proofreader, and all the staff in the Marketing Division for their support of this project.

- To *Carroll Collins* of HELPMECOOK® who proposed this project and coordinated the content, recipes, and photography for the cookbook. Without her passion and dedicated efforts, it would not have happened.

- To *"Team Blount"* at Blount Seafood for their very important partnership in producing Mohegan Sun Soups and Chowders:

  William Bigelow, Director of Research and Development

  Jeff Wirtz, Research and Development Chef

  Jens Retlev, Director of Culinary Development

  Kristin Bromley, Marketing Director

  Bob Sewall, Vice President of Sales & Marketing

  Todd Blount, President

  Captain Ted Blount

- To *Chris Vaccaro* of Chris Vaccaro Photography for the beautiful photographs throughout the book. To his assistants *John Tavares, Charles Estabrooks,* and *Ryan Bennet.* To *Cindy Salvato* of Cindy Salvato & Co. for her propping and food styling services.

- To *Ellen Hoverkamp* of Digital Imagery From My Neighbor's Garden for the spectacular scanner photography designed for the book's cover and endsheets.

- To *David Yandow* and *Todd Gianetti* of the Fowler & Huntting Company and to *Jennifer Martin* of The Hartford Food System for their continued support of local Connecticut farmers and independent growers.

- To the other members of the Mohegan Sun culinary family: *Todd English* of Tuscany, *Jasper White* of the Summer Shack, Michael Jordan's Steakhouse & Sports Bar, Big Bubba's BBQ and Johnny Rockets.

- To *Donna Cormier, Traci Racklyeft,* and *Deb Johnson* who keep the Food & Beverage Department organized and efficient.

- And finally, with the highest personal thanks, to the Chefs and Staff of Mohegan Sun—a legendary culinary team! Their talent, dedication, and desire to excel make it a pleasure to work with them.

My heartfelt thanks and gratitude to *Gary Crowder,* Senior Vice President, Food & Beverage and *Richard Zazzaro,* Vice President, Food & Beverage for their support and encouragement during the making of this book.

From all of us, we hope you enjoy *Under the Mohegan Sun*: A Celebration of Cuisine and Culture.

EXECUTIVE CHEF MICHAEL LUBOFF
Mohegan Sun

Contents

Contents

Mohe

The design for the Trail of Life is as old as memory.
Its curvilinear pattern serves as a guide for the journey of both
the individual and the Tribe, and it weaves its way through
the earthly and spiritual worlds alike. Its undulating curves reflect the
ups and downs of life itself but remind us that there is also an underlying
design to life. The dots along the way represent the people and plants
encountered during life's journey.

The Mohegan Trail
The Circle of Life
Traditional Foodways
Modern Foodways

Trail of Life

The Mohegan Trail

In the Mohegan cosmology, the earth was formed atop the back of a giant turtle known as Grandfather. Gunche Mundo, the Great Spirit, breathed a living spirit into all things: rocks, trees, plants, animals, and people, including the Lenni Lenape, or Real People. Eventually a clan which would become known as the Pequots/Mohegans separated from the other clans of Lenni Lenape and moved north-eastward and finally settled in Quinnetucket, present-day Connecticut.

There they found bountiful lands which provided venison, raccoon, bear, and fowl, as well as an abundance of nuts, wild fruits, ground nuts, and ground beans. The water of Long Island Sound and the many rivers and streams provided the most important protein sources of their diet—fish and shellfish. They planted corn and beans and enjoyed the lands in common as a gift of the Great Spirit.

A New England oral tradition says that an old chief saw what he described as a Great White Bird with outstretched wings arriving across the Great Water carrying strange-looking Pale Strangers. He foretold of the many changes that would take place with this arrival. The advent of trade for European technology and marvelous goods in exchange for furs and pelts would soon pit the English against the Dutch and create tensions within the Tribe for control and leadership.

Uncas

Uncas, the first Sachem of the Mohegans, led a group to separate from the larger Pequot clan and eventually move across the Pequot (Thames) River at Shantok, to settle on his family's traditional hunting territory. His followers kept their clan name of Mohegan, meaning Wolf People. The spirit of Mohegan lies at Fort Shantok today and the ancient Mohegan village site of Uncas is now on the National Historic Landmark register.

After the defeat of the Pequots, the Mohegan Tribe held territory from Long Island Sound to the Massachusetts border and from the Connecticut River east to the Pawcatuck River, which demarks the present-day boundary with Rhode Island. By the end of the seventeenth century, the Mohegan Tribe was the primary native political power in southern New England. Throughout the wars for the domination of North America, the Mohegans fought beside their neighbors against the French. During the American Revolution, Mohegans fought on the side of the rebels; a Mohegan was the first Native American to be killed at Bunker Hill. But by 1783, the Mohegans had only 2,700 acres of reservation left.

On March 30, 1831, Lucy Teecomewas and Cynthia Hoscoat—both Mohegan—conveyed a parcel of land on Uncas Hill which formerly was the property of their mother and grandmother, Lucy Occum Tantaquidgeon, to the Mohegan Tribe for the purpose of building a church. The title was to remain as tribal property as long as it was used for this purpose. It was the site of a Mohegan school and became the Tribe's social and political center as well as a religious gathering place. It is still open to the public for Congregational services.

The Mohegan land was divided up into individual plots in 1872. In 1978, the United States government created a process through which Tribes could petition for Federal Acknowledgement. The Mohegan Nation was formally recognized by the Federal Government on March 7, 1994, and in 1995, 240 acres of the northernmost traditional Mohegan reservation lands were repurchased by the Tribe and placed in trust by the United States government.

Today, the Mohegan number about 1,650 people. We have maintained a tribal structure with the single voice necessary to pursue justice in British, Colonial, and Federal courts. We gather yearly at the Green Corn Festival early in August. This homecoming is followed by the Wigwam Festival, which is open to the public and which gives us the opportunity to share some aspects of our culture with the community at large.

One of our current projects is the restoration of the Mohegan language. Although the last fluent speaker of Mohegan, Fidelia Fielding, died in 1908, reconstruction is being accomplished through collecting the known Mohegan words and comparing them with the Algonquin dialects of the people immediately around us and with the construction and usage of the language by those Tribes who still have fluent speakers. Through computer projection, we will be able to follow the development of the language through space and time. Our language group meets twice each month with the exception of August, and materials are available to those tribal members who are interested.

We are very exited about the opportunities we are able to provide to our People in education, health, and welfare. All Mohegans have the opportunity to go either to college or to vocational training. All are able to use the Tribal health insurance. Low-interest loans are available for those who want to start their own business. Housing is available for our Elders, and some members of the Tribe are provided subsidized housing.

Mohegans have long believed that the past, present, and future are inexorably linked and that one cannot exist without the others. Our ancestors form our roots to the Tree of Life, our living Tribe is the trunk, and our children and grandchildren are the buds of our future.

The Circle of Life

There are thirteen moons representing the thirteen lunar months in the Mohegan year. The year begins when the circle of life renews itself in the spring. Like many cultures, we mark the arrival of the new year with "sweetness," which in our case begins with the flowering of the maple sugar.

Maple Sugar Moon
The return of flocks of geese and other native birds is celebrated in this season. These winged beings are seen as messengers bringing omens from the Spirit World. This is also the season when the maple sugar runs. Maple was used as a sweetening agent and to make frames for dwellings, bowls, scoops, ladles, spoons, and stirring paddles. The inner bark was used to make a cough remedy.

Moon of the Peeping Frogs
Rain showers call the peeping frogs, who signal plants to sprout and blossoms to grow on the sassafras trees. We believe that you will continue to do throughout the year whatever you are doing when you hear the first spring peepers.

Moon of the Corn Planting
We hold in reverence the Spirit of Corn. It is planted when the moon is full, along with beans and squash—the Three Sisters. Squash leaves keep down weeds and corn stalks provide the beans with growing poles. In the symbol, seven women sing, dance, and make offerings to the seven hills of corn while men work their nets, weirs, and hemp lines for fishing.

Moon of the Strawberry
As the dogwood blooms, preparations are made for the feast of strawberries, the first of which are considered the most highly medicinal of all fruits. At the feast, young men and women begin their courtship ceremonies. Shadbush and dogwood blossoms also herald the shad fishing season.

Thunder Moon
The Thunder Moon announces the warm days of gathering the first blackberries and the first sweet corn that is believed to provide nourishment for the spirit as well as the body. At this season, young people make flags and sing songs to celebrate the first succotash, made from corn and pink beans.

Moon of the Hot Suns
This is the hottest time of the year, when gardens become dry and the people enjoy swimming in the river and digging for clams, a staple of our early diet. Their shells were carved into wampum beads, which were worn as a highly prized badge of honor and a guard against spiritual infection, rather than as money. This is the season of joyful celebration, when the people travel to ceremonial gatherings and enjoy times with old and new friends.

Harvest Moon

The harvest was a time of great feasting and thanksgiving, as the pumpkins were gathered along with the last of the corn, beans, and squash. This custom of thanksgiving at the Corn Harvest was renewed in 1860, when a woman had a dream in which the spirit of her mother told the people to return to it.

Moon of the Falling Leaves

As the harvest draws to a close, Mohegan hunters follow ancient practices in preparation for the months ahead. This is a magical time of crisp weather, when the autumn leaves turn brilliant colors and begin to fall. The colors of the leaves result when Ursa Major, the Great Hunter, kills and roasts Orion, the Sky Bear, constellations that are seen in the autumn sky.

Hunting Moon

As the frosts increase, the time for hunting deer begins, and young men are taught the lessons of how to conduct a respectful hunt. Deer was always a staple in the diet of the Mohegan, and the hunter is made aware of the ceremonial importance of the deer hunt.

Beaver Moon

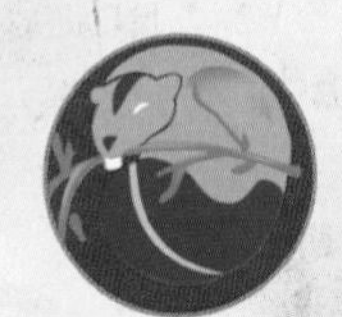

As the approach of winter is signaled, it is time to trap beaver, smoke meats, and perform the ceremony of burning deer bones to give thanks for a favorable hunt. Hunters shared game with their neighbors in the belief that all foods are the gift of the Creator and that the proper way to give thanks for blessings is by sharing them with others.

Wolf Moon

The wolf signifies the season of extreme cold when food is most scarce. More time is spent around the fire; smudgepots burn cedar and sweetgrass to cleanse the dwelling of bad spirits and to bring health and good spirits to those facing the long winter. The smoke carries thanks and requests to the Creator.

Cold Moon

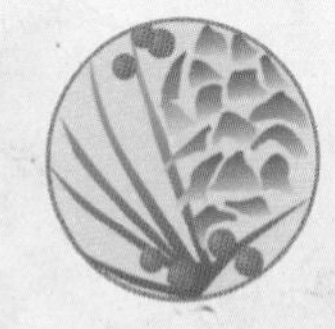

As the snow falls more often and the river freezes, the nights grow longer and the time of midwinter story telling begins. Tales of legendary ancestors are told beside the fire and games of chance are played to sort out the balance between the good and evil forces in the universe.

Moon of Snow Wading

If the moon becomes partially concealed by a hazy atmosphere, it is said that the moon is wading through snow. Claps of early thunder signal the oncoming thaw and the renewal of the circle of life.

Traditional Foodways

The Mohegan relied on foodways related to hunting, fishing, planting, and gathering. The names and symbols of the thirteen lunar months represent both the importance of each of these activities in the yearly calendar and the importance of their success to the continued survival of the Tribe. In each season, the proper ceremonies marked the Tribe's awareness of the balance that needed to be maintained with the natural world and their gratitude for its continued bounty as they planted, harvested, and hunted. Many different foods were enjoyed, but the combination of venison, shellfish, and corn formed the dietary and spiritual foundation of the Tribe's sustenance.

The Tribe members traditionally shared food, both with each other and with visitors, believing that to be the proper way to give thanks. There was always a pot of some kind of food on the fire if there were any food at all in the village, in order that neither Tribal member nor guest should ever go hungry. It can be assumed that the Mohegan people shared their knowledge of native plants, animals, and fowl with their new neighbors.

Wutáhim Wiyon

The main meal of the Mohegans was eaten several hours after rising, and it could be anything available and filling. Snacks would fill out the day as people went about their business, and a light meal was taken before bedtime.

It is conceded that corn was a primary staple of Indian life after its introduction to New England peoples about 1,000 years ago. It was thought to nourish the soul as well as the body. The planting of corn and other food crops is associated with spring, the beginning of the Mohegan calendar year, when the circle of life renews itself. It is a primary member of the foods known as the "Three Sisters"—corn, squash, and beans—because each crop helps the others to grown. Corn is used as a stake to support the bean plants. In addition, beans have nitrogen-fixing bacteria on their roots, which serve to enrich and fertilize the soil. Squash vines cover the ground in shade to keep the moisture in and the weeds out.

Mohegan legend has it that a crow brought them their first corn and beans from the garden of the Creator in the far off Southwest. That coincides with the historic record which tells us that corn was first developed from a grass in Mexico about 5,000 years ago. The corn traditionally grown by the Mohegans is the eight-row flint corn and is still grown by some today. They also grew a type of corn that was used specifically for popcorn, which was popped on the cob. It was planted far enough away from the main corn crop that the two did not cross-pollinate.

Accounts by settlers indicate that the ground was broken up and then heaped into hills about two or three feet apart for Indian corn planting. Fish would be added to each hill before planting, not just for fertilizer, but in order that the decaying fish would keep the earth warm and protect the seed against a late frost. Five or six kernels of corn were placed in each hill. When the corn was about four or five inches high, three or four dried beans were also placed in each hill. Some farm land in the area still bears evidence of these planting hills, which run in parallel rows and which still exhibit a greater fertility than the areas in between. Massapeag is one of the ancient Mohegan cornfields.

Corn was prepared and eaten in many ways, both fresh and dried. Fresh corn could be boiled for about six minutes in water. It could also be roasted by peeling the husks down and removing the silks, but keeping the husks attached. The kernels were rubbed with oil and the husks pulled back up over the oiled ear of corn. The ears were then soaked in water and roasted for twenty to twenty-five minutes. The same method is still used today on a grill rack.

Succotash

This recipe combines corn and beans in a manner traditionally used by the Mohegans. You can add chopped rabbit or fowl for a heartier one-dish meal. Add sliced Jerusalem artichokes for additional flavor and a thicker consistency.

3 tablespoons butter or minced salt pork
1 small onion, chopped
1 1/2 cups lima beans, pinto beans or other shell beans
1 1/2 cups fresh corn kernels
1/2 cup water
1/2 teaspoon pepper
1/2 cup cream

Melt the butter or cook the salt pork in a large skillet until the drippings are rendered. Add the onion and cook until translucent. Add the beans, corn, water and pepper. Cook, covered, for 10 to 15 minutes or until heated through. Stir in the cream and cook for 5 minutes longer. Serve hot.

The majority of the corn crop, however, was dried and stored in underground pits, wrapped in matting, for the long winter months. The hard (flint) shell on the kernels discouraged the corn from spoiling in storage. The dried kernels could be used whole in soups or they could be ground and mixed with suet and berries to use as a snack or traveling food, much like today's trail mix. The finest ground meal was sifted through a basket and made into bread. Historical records indicate that it was made into flat cakes about one inch thick, which were baked by burying them in hot ashes.

The second sister in the crop triumvirate was beans, eaten both fresh and dried, in the pod and shelled. Green beans were strung and hung in the sun to dry. They resembled breeches when hanging and were referred to as leather breeches. The dried beans were soaked in water before using them in stews and soups. Both the leather breeches and dried shelled beans could be stored to last through the winter months. In addition to succotash, other modern recipes reflect the traditional ways of preparing dried beans.

Three-Bean Casserole

1 pound dried soldier beans or Great Northern beans
1 pound dried lima beans or pea beans
1 pound dried kidney beans or black-eyed peas
1 large onion, chopped
1 garlic clove, chopped
1/2 cup ketchup or tomato purée
1 1/2 tablespoons cider vinegar
1/4 cup maple syrup
1 teaspoon dry mustard
salt and pepper to taste
3 slices bacon

Rinse and pick the dried beans. Combine with enough water to cover in a large saucepan and cook for 2 hours; drain. Combine the beans with the onion, garlic, ketchup, vinegar, maple syrup and dry mustard; season to taste and mix well. Spoon into a large baking dish and top with the bacon. Bake at 350 degrees for 1 1/2 hours. Serve hot.

The third sister was squash, and included both summer squash, winter squash, and pumpkin, which is also a squash. Several of these migrated from Central America along with corn, but others may have actually been first domesticated in the eastern part of North America. Pumpkin, like winter squash, can be used boiled, roasted, or dried in thin slices and then ground like cornmeal.

In addition to cultivated crops, Mohegans gathered fiddleheads and early sprouting skunk cabbage in the spring. They gathered cranberries, wild blueberries, wild strawberries, and "fox" grapes to eat fresh and to dry for use as sweeteners. Wild nuts and wild rice, which is really the seeds of a marsh grass that grows around freshwater lakes in the northern portions of the United States, were also dietary staples. For seasoning they used juniper berries, sassafras, sweet bay, black birch, maple and birch sugar, and the rendered drippings from raccoons and bear.

Cranberry-Stuffed Acorn Squash

Cranberries were one of the wild berries that the Mohegans gathered from areas near present-day Miller's Pond and Ashbow cemetery. Cranberries were later domesticated to become a staple New England crop.

4 small acorn squash
1 1/2 cups whole fresh or frozen cranberries
1/2 teaspoons grated orange zest
1/2 cup applesauce
1/2 cup maple sugar or brown sugar
1 tablespoon hazelnut oil

Cut each squash into halves and discard the seeds. Trim the ends so the halves will stand. Place cut side down in a baking dish and bake at 350 degrees for 35 minutes. Cool to room temperature. Combine the cranberries, orange zest, applesauce, maple sugar and hazelnut oil in a bowl and mix well. Spoon into the cavities of the squash. Place filled side up in a baking dish and bake for 30 minutes longer. Serve immediately. You may serve with whipped cream if desired.

Tumôhq Wiyon

Native American fishermen harvested fish both from canoes along the shores of the ocean and from the rivers. Salt water catches included the smaller fish as well as the occasional large fish, such as sturgeon. These were struck with a harpoon-like weapon, the head of which would remain in the fish; they would then be dragged to land by the cord or in nets made of wild hemp. Sometimes porpoises were trapped among the rocks or in the shallows, and evidence of shark, bluefish, cod, salmon, shad, and grouper were reported from one site. There is even evidence for the occasional killing of a whale.

New England rivers were known for their abundant supply of fish. The most effective method of catching fresh water fish was with weirs, some of which still exist. Weirs were constructed of stakes in the shallow portions of the rivers. A massive amount of labor was required to construct the weirs, but the equipment was very basic, and in spawning times the catch would have been enormous. This was especially important because it occurred at a time of the year when other plant and animal resources were at their lowest availability.

Steamed Fish and Wild Rice

6 ounces uncooked wild rice
1 cup water
2 cups broth
2 large bay leaves
6 juniper berries
pinch of cloves, ginger and paprika
1 1/2 pounds mild fish, such as flounder, cod or shad, cleaned and boned

Combine the wild rice with the water and 1 cup of the broth in a saucepan. Cook until tender and keep warm. Combine the remaining broth with the bay leaves, juniper berries, cloves, ginger and paprika in a large steamer. Bring to a boil and reduce the heat to simmer. Add the fish on a steamer tray above the broth and steam for 5 to 10 minutes or until the fish flakes easily. Serve over wild rice.

Summer was the primary season for fishing and gathering shellfish, both freshwater and saltwater. There were temporary camps at the shore during the summer to take advantage of the seafood, which was a major part of the Mohegan diet. The chapter of Tribal Soups includes several modern interpretations of traditional soups using fresh shellfish. Hundreds of huge shell middens in the area give testimony to the large-scale preservation of shellfish for the winter as well. To open oysters and clams, they placed a layer of rounded stones in an extended rectangular square or circle and built a large fire of hardwoods on the stones. When the fire burned down, the shellfish were placed in layers of seaweed over the hot stones and coals and steamed until they opened. The meat was then strung on lines in the sun to cure.

Clam or Mussel Chowder

3 cups chopped quahog clams or mussels
3 ounces salt pork, minced
1 large onion, chopped
4 large cooked potatoes, sliced at an angle and chopped
pinch of sage and thyme
3 cups broth

Drain the clams, reserving the juices. Cook the salt pork in a saucepan until the pork is brown and the fat has been rendered. Add the onion and sauté until translucent. Add the potatoes, clam meat, sage, thyme, broth and reserved clam juices. Cook until done to taste; the thinner pieces of potato will disintegrate to thicken the soup. Serve immediately or store in the refrigerator and reheat to serve.

The tribe hunted a variety of game and game birds including turkey, ducks, geese, deer, rabbits, squirrels, and even bears. There was a seasonal quality to hunting, focusing on game birds as they returned in the spring and larger game in the fall. These were roasted and broiled over open fires, or cooked in water using hot stones dropped into watertight vessels. Meat was also dried or smoked and stored for the long winter months when game was scarce.

Winter was the time for drawing on the resources that had been preserved during the year. Dried corn, beans, berries, game, fish, and shellfish were brought from storage to cook in pots over winter fires, and the people gathered around the fires to tell the tales of the Tribe and celebrate the gifts of the Creator.

Kipunumawôk Wiyon

Modern Foodways

Mohegan Aquaculture LLC became a commercial shellfish operation in 2002, when the U.S. Army Corps of Engineers approved a permit allowing the Tribe to grow shellfish at six sites in and around Long Island Sound. At that time the program was judged to be economically viable.

The six sites approved by the Corps of Engineers are in Niantic Bay, Fishers Island Sound, Pine Island Bay, Stonington Harbor, Long Island Sound, and the Pawcatuck River. Several sites were eliminated completely to protect environmental resources or recreational uses. The Tribe currently leases land from the Niantic Shellfish Commission and has several leases with the state of Connecticut.

Although the Tribe will use only a fraction of the 1,480 acres of underwater land it leases, the project is the largest venture of its kind ever undertaken in Connecticut. The permit allows the Tribe to install and maintain subsurface longlines on bottom cages and submersible surface bags for the growing of shellfish—specifically Eastern oysters, bay scallops, and hard clams. The young shellfish will mature in the leased sites; oysters grow in cages hanging below the surface, and clams grow on the bottom. They anticipate seeding the Niantic River with scallops.

The Tribe had first proposed the aquaculture venture in 1999, but scaled the project back when fishermen, boaters, and residents voiced concerns about potential obstruction to navigation and potential negative impact on marine life. The decision by the Corps of Engineers was arrived at after careful review and determination that the proposed project would not interfere with navigation and would have minimal impact on the marine environment.

Mohegan Sun is a strong supporter of the farming community in Connecticut. Partnering with local farmers and independent wholesalers, Mohegan Sun contracts for fresh fruit, produce, meats, and dairy products that are used throughout the on-site restaurants. Many of the chefs adjust their menus to showcase fresh, seasonal ingredients.

Each Wednesday during the summer, local growers are invited to display their products at a Farmers' Market held at the Mohegan Sun location. Thousands of Connecticut residents and Mohegan Sun visitors enjoy the festivities, which include the Fire Department Cook-Off and end with a spectacular fireworks display.

Each year, the proceeds of the cook-off are donated to a national charity. Past recipients have been the New York Uniformed Firefighters Widows' and Children's Fund in 2002, the National Red Cross Armed Services Emergency Fund in 2003, and Habitat for Humanity, ECHO, and HOPE in 2004.

The state of Connecticut also takes pride in marketing a variety of locally-grown agricultural and organic products and has initiated several projects to protect and support farming. For more information, contact the Connecticut Department of Agriculture online at www.ct.gov./doag.

Mohegan

Native ingredients were the inspiration for the tribal soups and chowders featured in this chapter. Ideas for these authentic Mohegan soups came from research into the history of the Tribe and the ingredients indigenous to southeastern Connecticut. They were developed by the chefs of Mohegan Sun, headed by Executive Chef Michael Luboff and Executive Sous Chef Craig Schmalz, using the freshest vegetables and seafood available from local sources. They are produced commercially in partnership with Blount Seafood of Warren, Rhode Island, and can be ordered directly (see page 159).

Tribal Soups

Chicken and Corn Chowder

5 tablespoons butter
1 cup chopped onion
$1/2$ cup chopped celery
$1/2$ cup chopped potato
5 tablespoons all-purpose flour
5 cups Chicken Stock *(below)*
2 cups Mohegan Corn Stock *(page 27)*
$1/3$ cup yellow corn
$1/3$ cup white shoepeg corn
$1/4$ cup chopped red bell pepper
$2/3$ cup chopped butternut squash
1 cup chopped cooked chicken
$1/4$ cup chopped dried cranberries
1 cup heavy cream
kosher salt and freshly ground black pepper to taste

Heat the butter in a large stockpot over low heat. Add the onion, celery and potato and cook until the onion and celery are tender, about 10 minutes. Stir in the flour and cook over low heat for 7 minutes.

Add the Chicken Stock and Mohegan Corn Stock gradually. Bring to a boil, stirring constantly. Add the yellow corn, white shoepeg corn, red bell pepper, butternut squash and cooked chicken.

Return to a boil and reduce the heat. Simmer for 45 minutes. Stir in the dried cranberries. Stir in the cream gradually and season with kosher salt and pepper.

Makes 10 servings

Chicken Stock

1 chicken, cut up
$4^1/2$ quarts cold water
3 onions, cut into quarters
1 tablespoon kosher salt
3 carrots, chopped
3 ribs celery, chopped
6 black peppercorns
2 sprigs dill
3 sprigs parsley

Rinse the chicken and pat dry. Combine with the cold water, onions and kosher salt in a large stockpot. Bring to a simmer over medium heat and cook for $1^1/2$ hours, skimming the surface occasionally.

Add the carrots, celery, peppercorns, dill and parsley. Cover and cook over low heat for 1 hour or until the chicken is tender, skimming occasionally. Remove the chicken and reserve for another use. Strain the stock through a fine mesh strainer.

Makes about 3 quarts

Mohegan Corn Stock

4 cups yellow corn
2 cups white shoepeg corn
4 quarts cold water
3 tablespoons sugar
1 tablespoon kosher salt

Combine the yellow corn and white corn with the cold water in a large stockpot. Add the sugar and kosher salt. Bring to a boil and reduce the heat. Cook until the liquid is reduced by 1/2.

Strain through a fine mesh strainer and reserve the corn for the Chicken and Corn Chowder or another use.

Makes 2 quarts

Hunter Stew

1/4 cup dried blue corn
1/4 cup vegetable oil
12 ounces cubed buffalo meat or beef
12 ounces pork, chopped
1/4 cup chopped onion
2/3 cup chopped carrot
2/3 cup chopped potato
2 cups chopped tomatoes
2 cups water
1/4 cup barbecue sauce
2 teaspoons cider vinegar
1/2 teaspoon Tabasco sauce
1/2 teaspoon dry mustard
1/2 cup Worcestershire sauce
1 teaspoon creole seasoning
1 teaspoon garlic powder
12 ounces chicken, chopped
2 cups Mohegan Corn Stock *(page 27)*
1/4 cup yellow corn
1/4 cup chopped red bell pepper
1/4 cup baby lima beans
1/4 cup chopped pearl onions
1/2 teaspoon freshly ground black pepper
3 tablespoons cornstarch
3 tablespoons water

Combine the blue corn with enough water to cover by 2 inches in a saucepan. Soak for 1 hour; drain.

Heat the vegetable oil in a large stockpot. Add the buffalo meat and pork and cook until browned. Add the onion, carrot and potato and sauté until tender, about 15 minutes. Add the blue corn, tomatoes and 2 cups water. Bring to a boil and reduce the heat. Simmer for 30 minutes.

Mix the barbecue sauce, vinegar, Tabasco sauce, dry mustard, Worcestershire sauce, creole seasoning and garlic powder in a bowl. Add to the simmering stew and stir to mix well. Add the chicken and Mohegan Corn Stock and cook for 10 minutes.

Stir in the yellow corn, red bell pepper, lima beans, pearl onions and pepper. Cook until the buffalo meat and blue corn are tender, about 30 minutes longer. Make a slurry with the cornstarch and 3 tablespoons water. Add to the stew and cook for 5 minutes, stirring constantly.

Makes 10 servings

Late Harvest Fruit and Vegetable Soup

3 tablespoons vegetable oil
1/4 cup chopped onion
1/4 cup chopped celery
1/4 cup chopped carrot
1/4 cup chopped potato
1/4 cup chopped parsnip
1/4 cup chopped turnip
1 cup chopped kale
1/4 cup chopped yellow squash
1/4 cup chopped butternut squash
1/4 cup chopped zucchini
1/2 cup mixed yellow and white corn
1/2 cup cranberry beans
7 cups Mohegan Corn Stock ***(page 27)***
1/3 cup tomato purée
1/2 cup cooked rice
2 tablespoons chopped dried apple
2 tablespoons chopped dried pear
1 teaspoon rubbed sage
3 tablespoons kosher salt
1 teaspoon white pepper

Heat the vegetable oil in a large stockpot. Add the onion, celery and carrot and sauté until tender, about 15 minutes.

Add the potato, parsnip, turnip, kale, squashes, zucchini and corn. Sauté for 10 minutes. Add the cranberry beans, Mohegan Corn Stock and tomato purée. Bring to a boil and reduce the heat. Simmer until the cranberry beans are tender but firm, about 30 minutes, adding additional Mohegan Corn Stock or water if needed for the desired consistency.

Add the cooked rice and dried fruit. Simmer for about 10 minutes or until the fruit is rehydrated. Stir in the sage, kosher salt and white pepper.

Makes 10 servings

Mohegan Clear Clam Chowder

24 quahog clams
2 tablespoons vegetable oil
6 slices bacon, chopped
1 cup chopped onion
1 cup chopped celery
1 cup chopped potato
5 cups clam juice
1 cup water
pinch of salt
1/2 teaspoon pepper

Wash and shuck the clams, reserving the juice. Chop the clams coarsely. Heat the vegetable oil in a large stockpot. Add the bacon, onion, celery and potato and sauté until the onion and celery are tender, about 15 minutes.

Add the reserved clam juice, the 5 cups additional clam juice and water. Bring to a boil, skimming the surface frequently. Add the chopped clams. Return to a boil and reduce the heat. Simmer for 10 minutes. Season with salt and the pepper.

Makes 10 servings

Oyster Chowder with Butternut Squash

24 oysters
1/2 cup (1 stick) butter
1/4 cup each chopped onion, celery and potato
3/4 cup all-purpose flour
4 cups Mohegan Corn Stock *(page 27)*
2 cups clam juice
1 cup chopped butternut squash
2 cups heavy cream
1 tablespoon salt
2 teaspoons white pepper

Wash and shuck the oysters, reserving the juice. Cut the oysters into halves. Heat the butter in a large stockpot over low heat. Add the onion, celery and potato and sauté until tender, about 15 minutes. Stir in the flour and cook for 7 minutes.

Add the Mohegan Corn Stock gradually and bring to a boil, stirring constantly. Reduce the heat and add the clam juice and reserved oyster juice. Add the butternut squash and cook until tender, about 15 to 20 minutes.

Add the oysters. Bring to a boil and reduce the heat. Stir in the cream gradually. Heat just to serving temperature; do not boil. Season with the salt and pepper.

Makes 10 servings

Smoked Onion and Wild Mushroom Soup

1/2 cup button mushrooms
1/2 cup cremini mushrooms
1/2 cup shiitake mushrooms
1/2 cup portobello mushrooms
2 leeks
1/4 cup vegetable oil
4 cups sliced white onions
6 shallots, sliced
1/4 cup burgundy wine
1/4 cup sliced celery
8 cups Mushroom Stock *(below)*
2 teaspoons chopped fresh thyme
2 teaspoons chopped fresh rosemary
1 tablespoon kosher salt
1 tablespoon cracked black peppercorns

Clean the mushrooms with a damp cloth or mushroom brush. Remove the stems and reserve for Mushroom Stock. Slice the mushroom caps. Clean the leeks and chop the white and light green portions only; reserve the darker green portions for Mushroom Stock.

Heat the vegetable oil in a large stockpot. Add half the onions and the leeks and shallots. Sauté until browned and well caramelized. Add half the mushrooms and sauté until tender and brown, about 8 to 10 minutes. Add the burgundy, stirring to deglaze the stockpot. Cook until reduced by 1/2.

Add the celery and remaining onions and mushrooms. Add the Mushroom Stock and bring to a boil. Reduce the heat and simmer for 30 minutes. Add the thyme and rosemary and season with the kosher salt and pepper.

Makes 10 servings

Mushroom Stock

stems from 2 cups mushrooms
green portions of 2 leeks, chopped
12 cups cold water
1 bay leaf
2 tablespoons salt
1 teaspoon whole peppercorns

Combine the mushroom stems and leek leaves with the cold water in a saucepan. Add the bay leaf, salt and pepper. Cook until reduced to 1/3. Strain the stock through a fine mesh strainer.

Makes 2 quarts

The casual dining restaurants in this chapter feature motifs derived from the traditional culture of the Mohegans. The designs in the restaurants include the Three Sisters of corn, beans, and squash, all of which are indigenous to the New England area and were the gift of nature from Native American agriculture to the world. Other scenes depict Mohegans sharing camaraderie and food with strangers just as they still do today, and the restaurants showcase the bounty native to the area.

Fidelia's
Mohegan Territory
Chief's Deli
The Cove

Comforts Today

Fidelia's is located adjacent to the hotel lobby
and is open twenty-four hours a day.
You will enjoy traditional hearty American fare in this light, open, and airy restaurant filled with swooping lines, wings and feathered finishes.

Vanilla Bean French Toast

Fruity Cheese Crepes

New England Turkey Burger

Delmonico Steak
Herbed Potatoes Sweet-and-Sour Onions

Mahogany Roasted Chicken
Jasmine Rice Lemon-Roasted Broccolini
Prawn Chips

Spicy Fried Rock Shrimp
Red Pepper Rémoulade

Vanilla Bean French Toast

6 eggs, or 12 ounces liquid egg substitute
1 vanilla bean, or 2 tablespoons vanilla extract
1/4 cup confectioners' sugar
1/2 cup half-and-half
24 slices egg bread
1/2 cup (1 stick) butter
1/2 pint fresh strawberries, sliced
1/2 pint fresh blueberries
confectioners' sugar
whipped butter
maple syrup

Whisk the eggs in a shallow dish. Split the vanilla bean and scrape the seeds into the eggs. Add 3/4 cup confectioners' sugar and the half-and-half; mix until smooth.

Dip each bread slice into the egg mixture for 10 seconds on each side, working in batches of 3 slices at a time.

Preheat a griddle to medium heat. Coat the griddle with 1 tablespoon of the butter. Place 3 slices of dipped bread onto the griddle at a time and cook until golden brown on both sides.

Stack the cooked slices of bread on a serving plate and cut the stack into halves. Repeat the process with the remaining bread, adding 1 tablespoon of butter to the griddle for each batch.

Top the French toast with the strawberries and blueberries. Dust with additional confectioners' sugar. Serve with whipped butter and warmed maple syrup.

Makes 8 servings

Fruity Cheese Crepes

MASCARPONE FILLING
6 ounces mascarpone cheese, softened
6 ounces cream cheese, softened
2 tablespoons confectioners' sugar
1 tablespoon heavy cream
1 teaspoon vanilla extract
1 banana, chopped
2 strawberries, chopped

CREPES AND ASSEMBLY
6 tablespoons vegetable oil
1 cup all-purpose flour
4 eggs
6 tablespoons whole milk
vegetable oil
blueberries, sliced strawberries and additional confectioners' sugar

To prepare the filling, combine the mascarpone cheese, cream cheese, 2 tablespoons confectioners' sugar, heavy cream and vanilla extract in a bowl; mix until smooth. Fold in the banana and strawberries. Spoon all but 1 cup of the mixture into a large pastry bag.

To prepare the crepes, combine 6 tablespoons vegetable oil, the flour, eggs and milk in a bowl and beat to form a smooth batter. Let stand at room temperature for 30 to 60 minutes.

Heat 1 tablespoon of vegetable oil in an 8-inch nonstick crepe pan. Ladle in enough batter to cover the bottom of the pan. Cook until set, turn and cook until lightly golden brown on the other side. Remove to a plate and keep warm. Repeat to make 12 crepes, adding additional vegetable oil if necessary.

Arrange the crepes on a clean flat surface. Pipe a small amount of filling from top to bottom in the middle of each crepe. Roll the crepes to enclose the filling.

Preheat the oven to 350 degrees. Arrange the crepes on a baking sheet. Bake for 3 minutes.

To assemble, spoon the remaining 1 cup of the filling into the pastry bag. Pipe a small dollop of filling onto the center of each serving plate. Arrange 3 crepes on each plate. Top with fresh blueberries, sliced strawberries and additional confectioners' sugar.

Makes 4 servings

New England Turkey Burger

3 pounds skinless white meat turkey, ground
1/2 cup chopped dried cranberries
1/2 small red onion, chopped
1/2 teaspoon dried sage
1/2 cup maple syrup
1/4 cup extra-virgin olive oil
kosher salt and freshly ground black pepper to taste
8 hamburger rolls, sliced and toasted
8 green lettuce leaves
16 beefsteak tomato slices
8 slices red onion

Combine the turkey, cranberries, red onion, sage, maple syrup and olive oil in a bowl. Season with kosher salt and pepper and mix well. Shape the mixture into 8 patties.

Spray a skillet or griddle with nonstick cooking spray. Add the patties and sear on both sides until cooked through and golden brown; juices should run clear when the patties are pierced.

Place each pattie on a toasted roll and top with lettuce, tomato and red onion. Serve with condiments.

Makes 8 servings

Delmonico Steak

Broccolini in Lemon Butter

1/2 cup (1 stick) butter, softened
1 tablespoon lemon juice
1/4 teaspoon kosher salt
1/2 teaspoon lemon pepper
2 1/2 pounds broccolini

Steaks and Assembly

8 (14-ounce) Delmonico ribeye steaks
salt and pepper to taste
Herbed Potatoes ***(page 41)***
Sweet-and-Sour Onions ***(page 41)***
chopped parsley for garnish

To prepare the broccolini, combine the butter, lemon juice, kosher salt and lemon pepper in a bowl and mix well.

Blanch the broccolini in boiling water for 1 minute; drain and plunge into ice water to stop the cooking process. Drain well. Melt the lemon butter in a saucepan and add the broccolini. Sauté for 3 minutes or until tender; keep warm.

To prepare the steaks, season them with salt and pepper. Grill until done to taste.

To assemble, spoon the Herbed Potatoes onto serving plates and place the steaks on the potatoes; top with the Sweet-and-Sour Onions. Arrange the broccolini on the side of each plate. Garnish the plates with parsley.

Makes 8 servings

Herbed Potatoes

3 1/2 pounds small Red Bliss potatoes
3/4 cup olive oil
1 tablespoon kosher salt
1 tablespoon white pepper
fresh thyme to taste
2 ounces Montreal seasoning

Preheat the oven to 400 degrees. Cut the potatoes into wedges. Pat dry with paper towels. Toss with the olive oil, kosher salt, white pepper, thyme and Montreal seasoning in a bowl. Arrange in a single layer on a baking sheet. Roast until fork tender, about 20 to 25 minutes.

Makes 8 servings

Sweet-and-Sour Onions

4 tablespoons red wine vinegar
1 cup red wine
4 tablespoons grenadine
3 tablespoons crème de cassis
kosher salt and freshly ground black pepper to taste
1 cup orange juice
4 medium red onions, thinly sliced

Combine the vinegar, red wine, grenadine, crème de cassis, kosher salt, pepper and orange juice in a saucepan and bring to a low boil. Add the onions and bring to a boil, stirring constantly. Reduce the heat and cook until reduced to a thick sauce, about 30 minutes. Adjust the seasonings.

Makes 8 servings

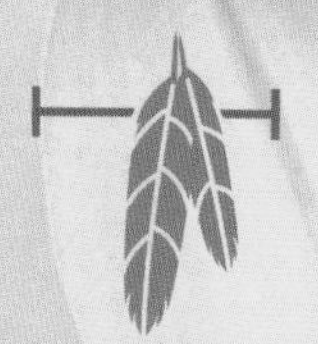

Mahogany Roasted Chicken

CHICKEN
1/2 cup hoisin sauce
1/2 cup oyster sauce
1/4 cup honey
2 tablespoons brown sugar
1 clove garlic, chopped
1 teaspoon chopped fresh gingerroot
1 teaspoon Chinese five-spice powder
2 tablespoons sherry
6 tablespoons sesame oil
1 tablespoon vegetable oil
4 roasting chickens, split into halves

CILANTRO BRUSH
1/2 cup sesame oil
1 ounce fresh gingerroot, chopped
1 clove garlic, chopped
2 tablespoons chopped cilantro

ASSEMBLY
Jasmine Rice ***(page 43)***
Lemon-Roasted Broccolini ***(page 43)***
Prawn Chips ***(page 43)***
chopped fresh chives

To prepare the chicken, combine the hoisin sauce, oyster sauce, honey, brown sugar, garlic, gingerroot, five-spice powder and sherry in a large bowl. Add the sesame oil and vegetable oil gradually, whisking constantly until smooth. Add the chicken and marinate, covered, in the refrigerator for 1 hour; drain, reserving the marinade.

Preheat the oven to 325 degrees. Place the chicken cut side down on a baking sheet and brush with the reserved marinade. Roast about 45 to 60 minutes or until cooked through and the juices run clear when pierced with a fork.

To prepare the cilantro brush, combine the sesame oil, gingerroot, garlic and cilantro in a bowl; mix well.

To assemble, spoon the Jasmine Rice into the centers of the serving plates. Place the chicken on the rice and brush with the cilantro brush. Place the Lemon-Roasted Broccolini on the side and top with the Prawn Chips and chives.

Makes 8 servings

Jasmine Rice

16 ounces uncooked jasmine rice
2 tablespoons butter
kosher salt and white pepper to taste

Cook the rice using the package directions. Toss with the butter, kosher salt and white pepper in a bowl.

Makes 8 servings

Lemon-Roasted Broccolini

2 1/2 pounds broccolini
6 tablespoons (3/4 stick) butter
1 tablespoon lemon pepper
grated zest and juice of 1/2 lemon
pinch of salt

Blanch the broccolini in boiling water for 1 minute; drain and plunge into ice water to stop the cooking process. Melt the butter in a sauté pan and the add the lemon pepper, lemon zest, lemon juice and salt. Add the broccolini and sauté until tender.

Makes 8 servings

Prawn Chips

8 cups vegetable oil for deep-frying
50 pieces shrimp-flavored prawn chips (See Note)

Heat the vegetable oil to 325 degrees in a large stockpot. Deep-fry the prawn chips in the hot oil until light brown and twice the uncooked size, about 1 minute. Transfer to paper towels to drain.

NOTE: Shrimp-flavored Prawn chips are available in Asian markets and can be found in the Asian section of most supermarkets.

Makes 8 servings

Spicy Fried Rock Shrimp

Rabbit Ears

1 French baguette, cut diagonally into 16 slices
1/2 cup olive oil
kosher salt to taste
8 ounces mozzarella cheese, shredded
freshly ground black pepper to taste

Wasabi-Ginger Marinade

1/4 cup rice wine vinegar
1 tablespoon chopped pickled gingerroot
2 cloves garlic, minced
1/2 cup packed brown sugar
1 tablespoon wasabi powder
1 tablespoon kosher salt
2 scallions, chopped
1/4 cup sesame oil
1/2 cup olive oil

Shrimp

2 pounds frozen rock shrimp, thawed
3 cups all-purpose flour
1 cup potato starch
8 cups vegetable oil for deep-frying
Red Pepper Rémoulade ***(page 45)***

To prepare the rabbit ears, preheat the oven to 350 degrees. Brush the bread with the olive oil and season with kosher salt. Place on a rack on a baking sheet. Sprinkle with the cheese and pepper. Bake until golden brown.

To prepare the marinade, combine the rice wine vinegar, gingerroot, garlic, brown sugar, wasabi powder, kosher salt and scallions in a bowl. Add the sesame oil and olive oil and whisk to mix well.

To prepare the shrimp, add the rock shrimp to the marinade and marinate, covered, in the refrigerator for 1 hour. Drain.

Combine the flour and potato starch in a mixing bowl and mix well. Add the shrimp and coat evenly. Heat the vegetable oil to 360 degrees. Deep-fry the shrimp in batches in the heated oil until cooked through and golden brown, about 3 to 4 minutes.

To serve, drizzle half the Red Pepper Remoulade into tall parfait glasses or other decorative glasses. Add two rabbit ears to each parfait glass and fill with cooked shrimp. Drizzle with additional Remoulade and top with a frisée salad with balsamic vinaigrette. Serve immediately.

Makes 8 servings

Red Pepper Rémoulade

2 red bell peppers
1 cup mayonnaise
1 tablespoon chopped fresh parsley
2 tablespoons chopped cilantro
2 tablespoons spicy brown mustard
kosher salt and freshly ground black pepper to taste

Preheat the broiler for 5 minutes. Place the red bell peppers on a baking sheet lined with foil. Roast until the skins begin to bubble and blacken. Continue to roast until the skin is charred, but the flesh is still firm, turning the peppers with tongs until evenly roasted.

Transfer the red bell peppers to a bowl and cover with plastic wrap or place in a brown paper bag. Let steam for about 10 to 15 minutes. Peel off and discard the charred skins. Chop the peppers coarsely, discarding the stems and seeds.

Combine the roasted red bell peppers with the mayonnaise, parsley, cilantro, mustard, kosher salt and pepper in a blender or food processor. Process until smooth.

Makes 8 servings

Day, night, or in the wee hours of the morning, the warm and inviting atmosphere speaks of homestyle New England cooking. Chefs serve up steaming plates of favorites featuring breakfast fare, seafood, pot roast, and roasted turkey, along with soups, salads, sandwiches, and burgers.

Hash and Eggs

Weeroum Omelet

Buttermilk Pancakes

Triple Crown Salad
Chicken Salad Shrimp Salad Tuna Salad

Mediterranean Cobb Salad

Grilled Maple-Glazed Salmon
Red Bliss Smashed Potatoes Roasted Vegetables

Baked New England Scrod
Herb-Roasted Yukon Potatoes Steamed Broccoli

Hash and Eggs

4 pounds corned beef, cooked and trimmed
1/2 cup (1 stick) butter, melted
1 cup chopped white onion
3 pounds potatoes, shredded
kosher salt and freshly ground black pepper to taste
24 large eggs
1 orange, sliced
chopped fresh chives

Grind the corned beef in a grinder with a large-hole plate. Melt 4 tablespoons of the butter in a large skillet. Add the onion and potatoes and cook until the onion is caramelized and the potatoes are light brown.

Add the remaining butter to the skillet. Add the corned beef and mix well. Season with kosher salt and pepper. Cook until the hash is golden brown, stirring occasionally. Cook the eggs to taste in a skillet. Spoon the hash onto serving plates and top each serving with 3 eggs. Garnish with a slice of orange and snipped chives. Serve immediately.

Makes 8 servings

Weeroum Omelet

(Forgotten Tribal Ancestor)

1 cup (2 sticks) butter, melted
4 ounces fresh spinach, washed and trimmed
8 ounces button mushrooms, sliced
8 ounces bacon, crisp-cooked and chopped
24 large eggs, beaten
pinch of kosher salt and white pepper
8 ounces (2 cups) shredded Monterey Jack cheese
8 ounces (2 cups) shredded Cheddar cheese
4 plum tomatoes, chopped
1 orange, sliced
chopped fresh chives

Preheat the broiler. Melt 2 tablespoons of the butter in a nonstick 8-inch sauté pan over medium-high heat. Add 1/2 ounce of the spinach, 1 ounce of the mushrooms and 1 ounce of the bacon. Sauté just until the spinach is wilted, about 30 seconds.

Add 3 beaten eggs to the sauté pan and season with kosher salt and white pepper. Cook until the eggs begin to set on the bottom, shaking the pan lightly until the eggs are barely dry on top; take care not to make scrambled eggs.

Flip the egg mixture to the other side with a spatula when the eggs are set on the top. Cook for about 1 minute longer. Flip the eggs back to the first side and top with 1 ounce of the Jack cheese and 1 ounce of the Cheddar cheese. Broil until the cheese melts. Repeat the process to make 8 omelets.

To serve, flip the omelets onto serving plates and top with the tomatoes, orange slices and fresh chives.

Makes 8 servings

Buttermilk Pancakes

4 cups all-purpose flour
5 teaspoons baking powder
4 teaspoons sugar
1 teaspoon salt
4 cups buttermilk
2 large eggs, beaten
1/2 cup water
2 tablespoons vegetable oil
confectioners' sugar to taste
8 strawberries, sliced
1/2 cup blueberries
maple syrup

Sift the flour, baking powder, sugar and salt into a large bowl. Add the buttermilk, eggs, water and oil and stir until blended. Do not over mix. Let the batter stand, covered, in the refrigerator for 30 minutes. Thin the batter with a small amount of water if it becomes too thick.

Preheat a large skillet or griddle over medium heat. Spray lightly with nonstick cooking spray or spread with a small amount of additional oil. Ladle the batter by 1/2 cupfuls into the skillet, working in batches. Cook until bubbles appear on the top. Turn the pancakes over and continue to cook until light golden brown, about 2 minutes. Garnish with confectioners' sugar, sliced strawberries and blueberries. Serve with warm maple syrup.

Makes 25 to 30 pancakes

Triple Crown Salad

heart of 1 head romaine, washed and trimmed
1 head iceberg lettuce, washed and trimmed
8 hard-cooked eggs, sliced ***(page 62)***
8 vine-ripened tomatoes, sliced
2 pounds Chicken Salad ***(below)***
2 pounds Shrimp Salad ***(page 51)***
2 pounds Tuna Salad ***(page 51)***
1 medium red onion, thinly sliced
salad dressing

Chop the lettuces into 1-inch pieces and toss in a bowl. Spoon onto 8 serving plates. Arrange the eggs and tomatoes in a decorative pattern around the plates.

Scoop 4 ounces each of the Chicken Salad, Shrimp Salad and Tuna Salad on top of the lettuce on each plate. Top with the onion. Serve with your favorite salad dressing on the side.

Makes 8 servings

Chicken Salad

1 1/2 pounds chicken breasts, cooked and chopped
1 rib celery, minced
3/4 cup mayonnaise
1/2 teaspoon kosher salt
1/4 teaspoon white pepper
1/2 teaspoon onion powder

Combine the chicken, celery and mayonnaise in a bowl and mix well. Season with the kosher salt, white pepper and onion powder. Refrigerate until ready to serve.

Makes 4 (8-ounce) servings

Shrimp Salad

- $1^1/_2$ pounds medium shrimp, cooked and chopped
- $^3/_4$ cup mayonnaise
- 2 tablespoons lemon juice
- $^1/_2$ teaspoon kosher salt
- $^1/_4$ teaspoon white pepper
- 1 sprig fresh dill, chopped

Combine the shrimp, mayonnaise and lemon juice in a bowl and mix well. Season with the kosher salt, white pepper and dill. Refrigerate until ready to serve.

Makes 4 (8-ounce) servings

Tuna Salad

- $1^1/_2$ pounds chunk light tuna
- 1 rib celery, minced
- $^3/_4$ cup mayonnaise
- 2 tablespoons lemon juice
- $^1/_4$ teaspoon white pepper
- $^1/_2$ teaspoon onion powder

Combine the tuna, celery, mayonnaise and lemon juice in a bowl and mix well. Season with the white pepper and onion powder. Refrigerate until ready to serve.

Makes 4 (8-ounce) servings

Mediterranean Cobb Salad

Marinated Chicken
8 (6-ounce) chicken breasts
4 ounces pesto

Marinated Vegetables
1/2 cup extra-virgin olive oil
1/2 cup balsamic vinegar
1 sprig fresh rosemary, chopped
1 sprig fresh thyme, chopped
2 cloves garlic, chopped
1 clove shallot, chopped
kosher salt and freshly ground black pepper to taste
8 (4-inch) portobello mushrooms, cleaned and stemmed
16 spears asparagus
8 (1/4-inch) slices red onion
16 baby carrots, peeled and trimmed, leaving some green top

Salad
8 ounces spinach, trimmed, washed and chopped
4 ounces pine nuts, toasted
8 ounces (1 cup) Italian salad dressing
1 pound smoked pork loin, cut into 1/4-inch strips
8 marinated artichoke hearts, cut into halves
8 ounces roasted red peppers, julienned
16 (1/2-inch) fresh mozzarella balls
8 ounces kalamata olives, pitted

To marinate the chicken, rinse the chicken breasts with cold water and pat dry. Combine with the pesto in a bowl and marinate, covered, in the refrigerator for 2 hours.

To prepare the marinated vegetables, preheat the oven to 350 degrees. Combine the olive oil, vinegar, rosemary, thyme, garlic, shallot, kosher salt and pepper in a bowl and mix well. Dip the mushrooms into the marinade and place round side down on a baking sheet. Bake for 10 minutes. Cool slightly and chill in the refrigerator. Cut into diagonal slices.

Combine the asparagus and red onion with the marinade and marinate for 15 minutes. Grill and cool. Blanch the carrots in boiling water for 2 minutes and then shock in ice water.

To prepare the salad, grill the chicken until cooked through. Slice diagonally and keep warm.

Toss the spinach, pine nuts and Italian salad dressing in a salad bowl. Top with grilled chicken slices, baby carrots, asparagus, portobello mushroom slices, smoked pork loin and artichoke hearts in a decorative spiral pattern. Top with the roasted red peppers and grilled red onions. Arrange the mozzarella balls and olives around the salad.

Makes 6 to 8 servings

Grilled Maple-Glazed Salmon

$1^{1}/_{2}$ cups pure Vermont maple syrup
$^{1}/_{2}$ cup Dijon mustard
4 pounds Atlantic salmon fillets
kosher salt and freshly ground black pepper to taste
$^{1}/_{2}$ cup (1 stick) butter
Red Bliss Smashed Potatoes ***(page 55)***
Roasted Vegetables ***(page 55)***
sprigs of fresh rosemary for garnish

Preheat the oven to 350 degrees. Combine the syrup and Dijon mustard in a mixing bowl; mix well. Set aside.

Season the salmon fillets with kosher salt and pepper. Place skin side up on the grill and grill for 1 minute. Turn the fish and position at a 90-degree angle to the first grill marks to create a diamond pattern. Grill for 1 minute longer.

Melt the butter in a baking pan in the oven. Arrange the fish in the pan. Bake for 10 minutes. Brush with the maple-mustard sauce and bake for 5 to 10 minutes longer or until the salmon is cooked through.

Serve with Red Bliss Smashed Potatoes and Roasted Vegetables. Garnish each serving with a sprig of rosemary.

Makes 8 servings

Red Bliss Smashed Potatoes

16 medium red bliss potatoes
1 cup (2 sticks) butter
6 tablespoons milk
kosher salt and white pepper to taste

Boil the potatoes in enough water to cover in a saucepan until tender, about 10 to 15 minutes. Drain the water. Add the butter, milk, kosher salt and white pepper and mash until smooth.

Makes 8 servings

Roasted Vegetables

8 ounces baby carrots, peeled and trimmed
2 medium zucchini, cut into half moons
2 medium yellow squash, cut into half moons
1 large red onion or Bermuda onion, cut into 1-inch pieces
8 ounces green beans, trimmed and cut into halves
3 cloves garlic, minced
1/2 cup olive oil
kosher salt and freshly ground black pepper to taste

Blanch the carrots in boiling water in a saucepan for 1 minute. Drain and shock immediately in ice water. Drain again.

Preheat the oven to 350 degrees. Combine the carrots with the zucchini, squash, onion, green beans, garlic and olive oil in a bowl and mix well. Season with kosher salt and pepper. Spread on a baking sheet and roast for 20 minutes or until the vegetables are brown and tender. Serve immediately.

Makes 8 servings

Baked New England Scrod

2 sleeves butter crackers, finely crushed
1/2 cup chopped fresh parsley
3/4 cup (1 1/2 sticks) butter, melted
1/4 cup Pinot Grigio, or other white wine
4 pounds center-cut scrod fillets
1/4 cup (1/2 stick) butter
3/4 cup Pinot Grigio, or other white wine
Herb-Roasted Yukon Potatoes *(page 57)*
Steamed Broccoli *(page 57)*
2 lemons, cut into quarters

Preheat the oven to 350 degrees. Combine the cracker crumbs, parsley, 3/4 cup butter and 1/4 cup wine in a bowl and mix well; the mixture should be crumbly and barely stick together when compressed.

Melt 1/4 cup butter in a baking dish. Place the fish fillets skin side down in the baking dish and top with the crumb mixture. Add 3/4 cup wine to the pan. Bake until the fish flakes easily and the crumb coating is golden brown, about 15 to 18 minutes.

Serve with Herb-Roasted Yukon Potatoes and Steamed Broccoli. Garnish with a lemon wedge.

Makes 8 servings

Herb-Roasted Yukon Potatoes

16 medium Yukon Gold potatoes with skins, cut into quarters
1 sprig fresh rosemary, trimmed and chopped
1 sprig fresh thyme, trimmed and chopped
1 clove garlic, minced
1/4 cup olive oil
kosher salt and freshly ground black pepper to taste

Preheat the oven to 350 degrees. Combine the potatoes with the rosemary, thyme, garlic, olive oil, kosher salt and pepper in a bowl and mix well. Spread on a baking sheet and roast for 30 to 45 minutes or until the potatoes are golden brown.

Makes 8 servings

Steamed Broccoli

4 bunches broccoli, washed, trimmed and cut into halves
1/2 cup (1 stick) butter, melted
kosher salt to taste

Place the broccoli in a steamer basket over boiling water. Cover and steam for 1 minute or until done to taste; drain. Brush with the butter, season with kosher salt and serve.

Makes 8 servings

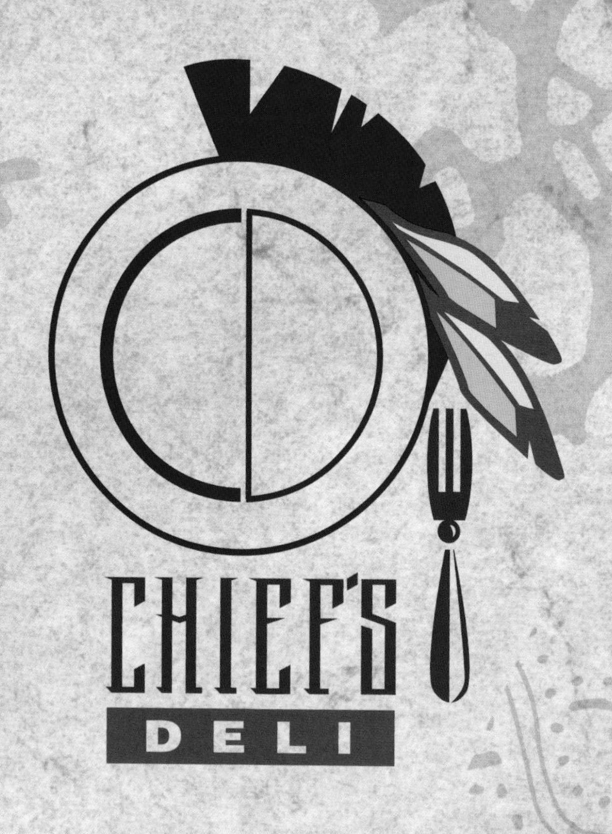

Break for lunch in our New York-style delicatessen, complete with old-fashioned counter service. Through our open kitchen, you will have a perfect view as sandwich chefs create taste sensations from freshly-sliced corned beef, pastrami, or other deli meats. A selection of hearty platters complements the sandwiches and salads, including mouthwatering desserts.

Matzo Ball Soup

Sweet-and-Sour Cabbage Soup

Chilled Maine Lobster Salad

Spinach Salad

Corned Beef Reuben

Potato Knishes

Cheddar Cheese and Parsley Biscuits

Matzo Ball Soup

MATZO BALLS
1 tablespoon salt
4 large eggs
1/4 cup vegetable oil
white pepper to taste
1 teaspoon onion powder
1 tablespoon baking powder
1/2 teaspoon salt
1 1/3 cups matzo meal

SOUP
8 cups Chicken Stock ***(page 26)***
3 large ribs celery, chopped
2 carrots, chopped
1 white onion, cut into quarters
kosher salt and white pepper to taste
pinch of chopped fresh dill

To prepare the matzo balls, fill a large wide stockpot three-quarters full with water. Add 1 tablespoon salt and bring to a boil.

Beat the eggs in a mixing bowl. Add the vegetable oil, white pepper, onion powder, baking powder, 1/2 teaspoon salt and matzo meal and mix well.

Shape into 1 1/4-inch balls with wet hands; the balls will double in size as they cook. Place gently in the boiling water. Reduce the heat and simmer for 25 minutes.

To prepare the soup, combine the Chicken Stock, celery, carrots and onion in a saucepan and bring to a boil. Reduce the heat, cover and simmer for 20 minutes. Remove the onion with a slotted spoon. Season with kosher salt, white pepper and fresh dill. Let stand for 5 minutes.

Remove the matzo balls from the cooking liquid with a slotted spoon and place 1 or 2 in each soup bowl. Ladle the soup into the bowls. Serve immediately

NOTE: Egg noodles can be added if desired.

Makes 8 servings

Sweet-and-Sour Cabbage Soup

1/2 cup vegetable oil
2 pounds chuck stew beef, cut into 1-inch cubes
1 teaspoon kosher salt
1/2 teaspoon white pepper
1 large onion, cut into 1/2-inch pieces
4 cloves garlic, chopped
1 (28-ounce) can whole peeled plum tomatoes
1 (28-ounce) can crushed tomatoes
1 cup ketchup
6 cups beef stock
1 cup sugar
juice of 1 lemon
1 teaspoon kosher salt
1 teaspoon white pepper
1 large head cabbage, cut into 1-inch pieces

Heat the vegetable oil in a large stockpot over medium-high heat. Season the stew beef with 1 teaspoon kosher salt and 1/2 teaspoon white pepper. Add to the stockpot, taking care not to crowd in the stockpot. Cook for 5 to 7 minutes or until seared on all sides. Add the onion and garlic and continue to cook for 5 to 7 minutes or until the onion begins to brown.

Add the whole tomatoes, crushed tomatoes, ketchup, beef stock, sugar, lemon juice, 1 teaspoon kosher salt and 1 teaspoon white pepper. Bring to a boil, then lower the heat and simmer for 1 hour.

Add the cabbage and cook for 15 minutes longer. Let stand until cool and store in the refrigerator for 24 hours to allow the flavors to blend. Reheat over low heat to serve. This is good served with mashed potatoes and buttered rye bread.

Makes 4 quarts

Chilled Maine Lobster Salad

2 pounds cooked lobster meat
3 or 4 ribs celery, chopped
1/2 teaspoon onion powder
1 tablespoon fresh lemon juice
1/2 cup mayonnaise
kosher salt and white pepper to taste
8 New England-style rolls
crisp lettuce

Drain any excess liquid from the lobster meat and chop the meat into bite-size pieces. Combine with the celery, onion powder and lemon juice in a bowl and toss to mix well. Stir in the mayonnaise and season with kosher salt and white pepper. Serve on the rolls and add crisp lettuce.

NOTE: You may also serve this on top of a fresh garden salad.

Makes 8 servings

Spinach Salad

SWEET-AND-SOUR DRESSING
1/2 cup ketchup
3 tablespoons brown sugar
1 cup balsamic vinegar
2 cups extra-virgin olive oil
cayenne pepper to taste

SALAD
16 ounces leaf or baby spinach
1 large red onion, sliced into rings
1 large tomato, chopped
10 ounces mushrooms, sliced
3 hard-cooked eggs, coarsely chopped (see Note)
grilled chicken breast or jumbo shrimp

To prepare the dressing, blend the ketchup and brown sugar in a bowl. Stir in the vinegar. Add the olive oil gradually, whisking until the dressing is smooth. Season with cayenne pepper.

To prepare the salad, mound the spinach in a large salad bowl. Arrange a ring of onion slices around over the top. Sprinkle with the tomato and mushrooms. Top with the hard-cooked eggs. Add grilled chicken or shrimp if desired. Drizzle with the dressing and serve.

NOTE: To hard-cook eggs, place them in a pan with enough cold water to cover. Bring to a rolling boil and reduce the heat to low. Cook for 20 minutes. Drain and rinse with cold water; cool.

Makes 6 servings

Corned Beef Reuben

RUSSIAN DRESSING
1/2 cup mayonnaise
1/4 cup ketchup
1 teaspoon Worcestershire sauce
1 tablespoon pickle relish
kosher salt and freshly ground black pepper to taste

SANDWICH
2 slices deli rye bread
softened butter for spreading
4 slices Swiss cheese
2 ounces sauerkraut
6 ounces corned beef, very thinly sliced, warmed

To prepare the dressing, combine the mayonnaise, ketchup, Worcestershire sauce and pickle relish in a bowl and mix well. Season with kosher salt and pepper. Chill until serving time.

To prepare the sandwich, coat one side of each piece of bread with a thin layer of butter. Place butter side down on a griddle or in a large skillet. Spread 2 tablespoons Russian Dressing on each slice of bread. Place 2 slices of cheese on each piece and top one slice with sauerkraut. Grill until golden brown. Top the other slice with the corned beef and press the two halves together.

Makes 1 serving

Potato Knishes

2 pounds Yukon Gold potatoes, peeled
1/2 cup milk
2 tablespoons butter
kosher salt and white pepper to taste
1 medium onion, finely chopped
3 tablespoons chopped parsley
2 tablespoons chopped scallions
Cheddar Cheese and Parsley Biscuit Dough *(page 65)*
2 eggs, beaten

Boil the potatoes in enough water to cover in a saucepan until tender. Drain well. Combine with the milk, 1 tablespoon butter, kosher salt and pepper in a large mixing bowl. Mash together until no lumps remain.

Melt the remaining 1 tablespoon butter in a sauté pan and add the onion. Sauté until translucent, about 8 to 10 minutes, taking care not to burn. Add to the potatoes with the parsley and scallions. Season with kosher salt and pepper to taste. Mix well.

Scoop the mixture into 2-ounce balls and place on a baking sheet. Place in the freezer for 1 hour.

Preheat the oven to 350 degrees. Remove the potato balls from the freezer and wrap each with a thin layer of biscuit dough. Brush the outside with the egg and place on a nonstick baking sheet. Bake for 20 to 25 minutes. Serve with sour cream and applesauce if desired.

Makes 20 knishes

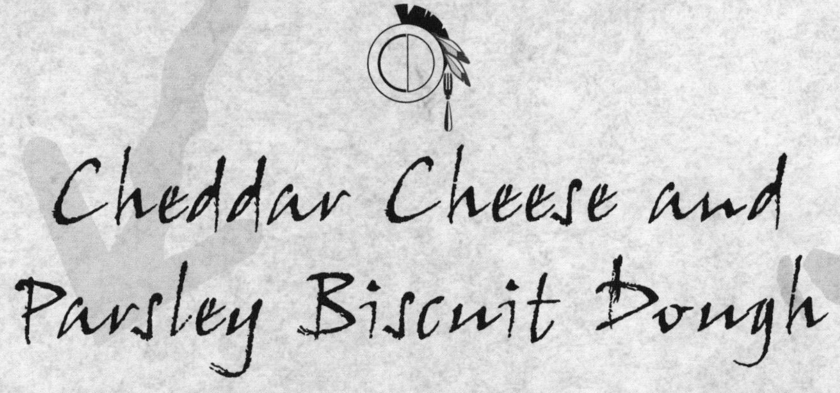

Cheddar Cheese and Parsley Biscuit Dough

1 1/3 cups all-purpose flour
1 tablespoon baking powder
1 teaspoon salt
2 tablespoons sugar
1 cup (2 sticks) plus 2 tablespoons cold butter, cubed
1 1/4 cups milk
8 ounces (2 cups) shredded Cheddar cheese
3 tablespoons chopped fresh parsley

Combine the flour, baking powder, salt, sugar and butter in a mixing bowl and mix until small crumbs form. Add the milk, cheese and parsley and mix to form a dough. Shape into a ball and let rest for 20 minutes.

Roll the dough thin on a lightly floured surface. Cut into circles large enough to enclose the frozen potato knishes.

You may also roll or pat the dough about 1/2 inch thick, cut into circles and bake for biscuits.

Makes 20 knishes

the cove

One of best-kept secrets at the Mohegan Sun, The Cove is located just outside three fine dining restaurants—The Longhouse, Pompeii & Caesar, and Bamboo Forest—and offers the opportunity to sample dishes from those restaurants at a great price. It also offers a dining experience unlike any other with its unique display kitchens that allow you to watch your meal being prepared from a comfortable bar stool.

Japanese Udong Noodle Soup

Lobster Bisque

Shellfish Bouillabaisse
Marinara Sauce Saffron Rouille

Shrimp Fra Diavolo

Margherita Pizza

Steak Fritte with French Fries

Saigon Beef Lettuce Wraps with Dan Dan Sauce

Pasta Fagioli

Japanese Udong Noodle Soup

SEAFOOD DUMPLINGS
1/2 cup uncooked shrimp
1/2 cup scallops
6 tablespoons fish sauce
1/2 cup fish paste
6 tablespoons hoisin sauce
6 tablespoons soy sauce
1/2 teaspoon ground ginger
8 won ton wrappers

SOUP
12 cups Chicken Stock, heated ***(page 26)***
8 ounces calamari
1 pound Chinese broccoli, chopped
1 pound small shrimp
8 ounces scallops
8 ounces fish cake, sliced
48 ounces uncooked udong noodles
4 scallions, chopped for garnish

To prepare the dumplings, finely chop the shrimp and scallops. Combine the shrimp and scallops with the fish sauce, fish paste, hoisin sauce, soy sauce and ginger in a mixing bowl and mix well. Spoon onto the won ton wrappers. Fold each wrapper to enclose the filling and seal. Cook in simmering water in a saucepan for 4 to 5 minutes; drain.

To prepare the soup, bring the Chicken Stock to a boil in a large stockpot. Add the calamari, broccoli, shrimp, scallops and fish cake and cook for 3 to 5 minutes. Reduce the heat to a simmer. Add the noodles and cook for 3 minutes longer.

To serve, place one dumpling in the bottom of each serving bowl. Ladle the soup over the dumplings and garnish with chopped scallions.

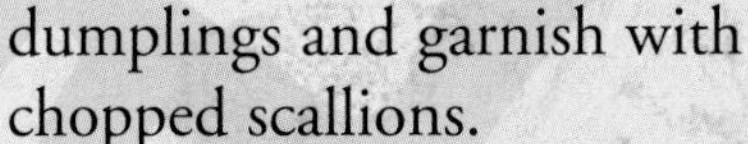

Makes 8 servings

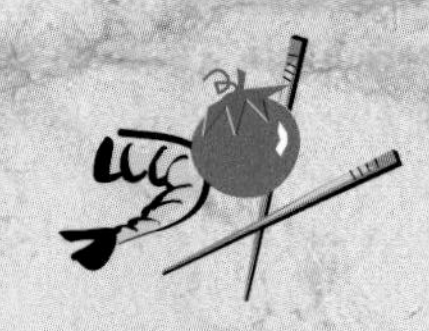

Lobster Bisque

6 tablespoons (3/4 stick) unsalted butter
6 tablespoons all-purpose flour
6 cups Lobster Stock ***(page 69)***
cooked lobster meat from 2 (1 1/2-pound) lobsters, chopped ***(page 69)***
4 cups heavy cream (see Note)
1/2 cup dry or sweet sherry
2 tablespoons cornstarch
1/4 cup water
kosher salt and freshly ground black pepper
fresh dill or parsley for garnish

Melt the butter in a large saucepan or stockpot and stir in the flour. Cook over low heat to form a roux, stirring constantly. Stir in the Lobster Stock, lobster meat, cream and sherry gradually. Simmer over low heat for 10 to 15 minutes or until the bisque begins to thicken, stirring frequently to avoid burning.

Blend the cornstarch with the water to make a slurry. Stir into the bisque and cook for 5 to 6 minutes longer or until thickened, stirring constantly. Season with kosher salt and pepper to taste. Let the bisque rest for 5 minutes before serving. Garnish with a sprig of dill or chopped parsley.

NOTE: You may omit the slurry of cornstarch and water if you prefer a thinner bisque. Heavy cream will ensure a rich and creamy bisque, but you can substitute light cream or half-and-half for a lighter version. You can also use the bisque as a wonderful sauce for seafood or crab cakes.

Makes 8 to 10 servings

Lobster Stock

1 large yellow onion, coarsely chopped
3 or 4 ribs celery with leaves, coarsely chopped
2 or 3 carrots, peeled and coarsely chopped
1/4 cup tomato paste
3 sprigs dill
3 sprigs parsley
2 to 3 tablespoons kosher salt or sea salt
4 or 5 whole black peppercorns
2 (1 1/2-pound) live lobsters

Add enough water to a large stockpot to cover the lobsters by 1 or 2 inches. Add the onion, celery, carrots, tomato paste, dill, parsley, kosher salt and peppercorns to the water and bring to a boil.

Add the lobsters head first to the boiling water and return the water to a simmer. Simmer for 20 minutes. Remove the lobsters and strain the stock through a fine mesh strainer; discard the solids.

Crack the lobster shells; remove and chop the meat. Reserve the meat for the Lobster Bisque (page 68).

Combine the shells with the stock in the stockpot and bring to a slow simmer over low heat. Simmer for 1 hour, adding additional water if necessary; stock should measure 6 cups at the end of the cooking period.

Drain the stock again through a fine mesh strainer, discarding the shells. Adjust the salt to taste.

Makes 6 cups

Shellfish Bouillabaisse

40 littleneck clams
32 mussels
16 large shrimp
16 langoustines (optional)
16 crab claws
2 cloves garlic, chopped
1/4 cup olive oil
1 cup white wine
2 quarts Fish Stock ***(page 71)***
1/2 cup Marinara Sauce ***(page 71)***
16 slices toasted French bread
Saffron Rouille ***(page 71)***

Sauté the clams, mussels, shrimp, langoustines, crab claws and garlic in the olive oil in a large stockpot for 5 minutes, stirring to keep from burning. Deglaze the pan with the white wine. Add the Fish Stock and Marinara Sauce. Cook until the seafood is cooked through and the clam and mussel shells open up, discarding any unopened shells.

To serve, ladle the bouillabaisse into wide-mouth bowls. Top each serving with 2 slices of toasted French bread and drizzle the saffron rouille over the bread.

Makes 8 servings

Fish Stock

1 medium onion, coarsely chopped
3 ribs celery, coarsely chopped
3 leeks, white and light green portions only, cleaned and coarsely chopped
2 shallots, chopped
2 cloves garlic, chopped
1 tablespoon olive oil
8 cups cold water
8 ounces fish bones
1 teaspoon thyme
1 teaspoon black peppercorns
1 bay leaf
$1/4$ teaspoon saffron

Sauté the vegetables in the olive oil in a large saucepan. Add the remaining ingredients. Bring to a boil and reduce the heat. Simmer for 30 minutes. Strain the stock, discarding the solids.

Makes 2 quarts

Marinara Sauce

2 medium onions, chopped
2 tablespoons olive oil
32 ounces crushed plum tomatoes
1 tablespoon tomato paste
1 clove garlic, chopped
$1/2$ teaspoon chopped fresh basil
$1/2$ teaspoon oregano
1 teaspoon sugar
kosher salt and freshly ground black pepper to taste

Sauté the onions in the olive oil in a saucepan. Add the tomatoes, tomato paste, garlic, basil, oregano, sugar, kosher salt and pepper and bring to a boil. Reduce to a simmer and simmer for $2^1/2$ hours.

Makes 4 cups

Saffron Rouille

1 cup Fish Stock *(above)*
$1/4$ teaspoon saffron
2 slices French bread
1 clove garlic
kosher salt and pepper to taste
$1/4$ cup olive oil

Heat the Fish Stock in a saucepan; add the saffron and allow to steep. Pour into a food processor or blender. Add the French bread and garlic and season with kosher salt and pepper. Process until smooth. Add the olive oil and process until emulsified.

Makes 8 servings

Shrimp Fra Diavolo

1 cup olive oil
32 large shrimp, peeled and deveined
1/2 cup chopped garlic
red pepper flakes to taste
1 cup white wine
2 cups chopped plum tomatoes
4 cups Marinara Sauce *(page 71)*
1/4 cup chopped fresh basil
2 pounds uncooked spaghetti
8 slices French bread
8 ounces Garlic Butter *(page 75)*

Heat the olive oil in a saucepan. Add the shrimp, garlic and pepper flakes. Sauté for 5 minutes or until the shrimp are pink and cooked through. Deglaze pan with the wine. Add the tomatoes, Marinara Sauce and basil. Simmer for 3 to 4 minutes.

Cook the spaghetti using the package directions; drain. Toss the spaghetti with the shrimp mixture in a large bowl. Serve with the French bread slices and Garlic Butter.

Makes 8 servings

Margherita Pizza

1 recipe Pizza Dough *(below)*
1 tablespoon pesto
3/4 cup (3 ounces) shredded mozzarella cheese
2 or 3 plum tomatoes, sliced
6 to 8 basil leaves, cut chiffonade, for garnish

Preheat the oven to 450 degrees. Roll the Pizza Dough to a 16-inch circle on a lightly floured surface and spread with the pesto. Sprinkle with the cheese and arrange the tomatoes over the top.

Place the pizza on a pizza stone or pan and bake for 6 minutes or until the dough is crisp and the cheese is bubbly. Garnish with fresh basil.

Makes 1 pizza

Pizza Dough

1 1/2 teaspoons active dry yeast
9 ounces warm water
7 ounces high-gluten flour
1/2 teaspoon kosher salt
1 teaspoon sugar
1 teaspoon canola oil or olive oil

Whisk the yeast into the water in a bowl and set aside. Mix the flour, salt and sugar in a food processor fitted with a paddle. Add the canola oil and then the yeast mixture and mix at low speed. Increase the speed to medium and mix until the dough forms a ball and the sides of the bowl are clean. Let the dough rest, covered with a damp towel, at room temperature for 1 hour.

Makes 1 (16-inch) pizza crust

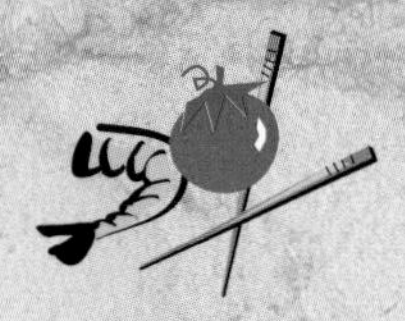

Steak Fritte with French Fries

Steaks
8 (8-ounce) sirloin steaks
1 cup olive oil
1 cup balsamic vinegar

French Fries
6 large russet potatoes
canola oil or peanut oil for deep-frying
kosher salt to taste

Assembly
32 ounces mesclun greens or spring mix
1/2 cup olive oil
1/4 cup white balsamic vinegar
kosher salt and freshly ground black pepper to taste
Garlic Butter ***(page 75)***
2 tablespoons chopped fresh chives

To prepare the steaks, pound them 1/4-inch thick. Combine the olive oil and vinegar in a bowl and add the steaks. Marinate at room temperature for 30 minutes; drain. Grill the steaks to desired doneness.

To prepare the French fries, peel the potatoes if desired and cut lengthwise into 1/2-inch slices. Cut the slices to 1/2-inch strips.

Heat the oil to 350 degrees in a deep fryer. Pat the potatoes dry with paper towels and deep-fry in the hot oil for about 4 to 5 minutes. Remove from the oil and spread on a rack to cool.

Increase the temperature of the oil to 375 degrees. Return the potatoes to the oil and deep-fry for about 4 minutes longer or until golden brown. Remove from the oil and drain well on paper towels. Season with kosher salt.

To assemble, toss the mesclun with the olive oil and vinegar in a bowl. Season with kosher salt and pepper. Cut the steaks into long strips and place in a large mixing bowl. Add the French fries, Garlic Butter and chives and toss to mix well. Mound on serving plates. Spoon the salad greens on the side.

Makes 8 servings

Garlic Butter

1 pound (4 sticks) butter, softened
1 head garlic, chopped
2 tablespoons chopped fresh parsley

Combine the butter with the garlic and parsley in a bowl. Beat until the garlic and parsley are incorporated and the butter is light and airy.

Makes 2 cups

Saigon Beef Lettuce Wraps with Dan Dan Sauce

Mirin Sauce
2 cups mirin wine
1 cup rice wine vinegar
1 tablespoon minced garlic
1 tablespoon minced gingerroot
1 teaspoon minced dried chile or garlic chili sauce
1 teaspoon sugar
1/2 cup fish sauce

Dan Dan Sauce
5 tablespoons soy sauce
5 tablespoons chili sauce
2 tablespoons chili oil (optional)
2 teaspoons chicken bouillon granules
3 tablespoons sugar
1/4 cup sesame paste
1/4 cup peanut paste
1 cup hoisin sauce

Beef Lettuce Wraps
4 pounds flank steak, shaved
1/2 cup sesame oil
5 ounces peanuts, chopped
2 heads iceberg lettuce, separated into leaves
8 ounces bean sprouts
4 ounces scallions, chopped

To prepare the mirin sauce, combine the mirin, wine vinegar, garlic, gingerroot, dried chile, sugar and fish sauce in a saucepan and mix well. Bring to a simmer and cook until reduced to 2 cups.

To prepare the dan dan sauce, combine the soy sauce, chili sauce, chili oil, bouillon, sugar, sesame paste, peanut paste and hoisin sauce in a large bowl and mix well.

To prepare the beef lettuce wraps, sauté the flank steak in the sesame oil and 1 1/3 cups of the dan dan sauce in a skillet. Sprinkle with the peanuts.

Spoon onto the lettuce leaves and top with the bean sprouts and scallions. Roll the lettuce leaves to enclose the filling. Serve with the mirin sauce.

Makes 8 servings

Pasta Fagioli

- 1½ cups dried Great Northern or cannellini beans
- 5 ounces pancetta, coarsely chopped
- ½ cup olive oil
- 2 medium onions, chopped
- 2 medium carrots, chopped
- 5 ribs celery, chopped
- 1 medium tomato, chopped
- 12 cups Chicken Stock *(page 26)*
- 1 teaspoon chopped fresh thyme
- 1 teaspoon chopped fresh rosemary
- 1 teaspoon chopped fresh oregano
- 1 head roasted garlic (see Note)
- kosher salt and freshly ground black pepper to taste
- 6 ounces ditalini, or other small shaped pasta, cooked
- celery leaves for garnish

Soak the beans overnight in enough cold water to cover in a bowl; drain. Cover with fresh water in a saucepan and cook until tender; drain.

Sauté the pancetta in the olive oil in a skillet for 2 minutes. Add the onions, carrots and celery and cook for 5 minutes.

Transfer to a stockpot and add the tomato, Chicken Stock, thyme, rosemary, oregano, roasted garlic and cooked beans. Season with kosher salt and pepper. Simmer for 45 minutes.

Chill for 24 hours if possible for optimum flavor. Reheat at serving time and ladle into wide, shallow bowls. Spoon the ditalini into the center and garnish with celery leaves.

NOTE: To roast garlic, slice the top off a head of garlic and place cut side up in a small baking dish. Drizzle 1 teaspoon extra-virgin olive oil over the top. Cover with foil and bake at 350 degrees for 30 minutes. Remove the foil and bake for 20 to 30 minutes longer. Cool. Squeeze the garlic from the cloves for use in cooking or as a delicious spread on crackers, breads or baked potatoes.

Makes 8 to 10 servings

The restaurants popular for evening dining feature both traditional Mohegan motifs, such as the ones celebrating the annual hunts in The Longhouse, as well as motifs that reflect the wider range of culinary sophistication of modern-day Mohegans and their visitors. They include cuisine from Italy to Asia, and all feature seasonal fare, with many of the same foods traditionally enjoyed by Mohegans presented with an international flourish.

Rain

Todd English's Tuscany

Pompeii and Caesar

Bamboo Forest

The Longhouse

After Dark

Rain is a sleek, sophisticated atmosphere for gourmet Continental dining, surrounded by cascading water, polished metals, glass ceramic "puddles" and shimmering surfaces. The restaurant interior creates an intimate setting reminiscent of a gentle summer rain.

Spring Pea Soup with Carrot Foam

Spring Veal Chops with Peas and Carrots
Vermouth Jus Parmesan Risotto

Colorado Lamb Rack with Peruvian Potatoes
and Spring Ratatouille

Gulf Snapper with Lobster Tomato Marinara
and Vegetable Cassoulet
Mushroom Risotto

Oysters Three Ways

Rabbit Confit with Goat Cheese Dumplings

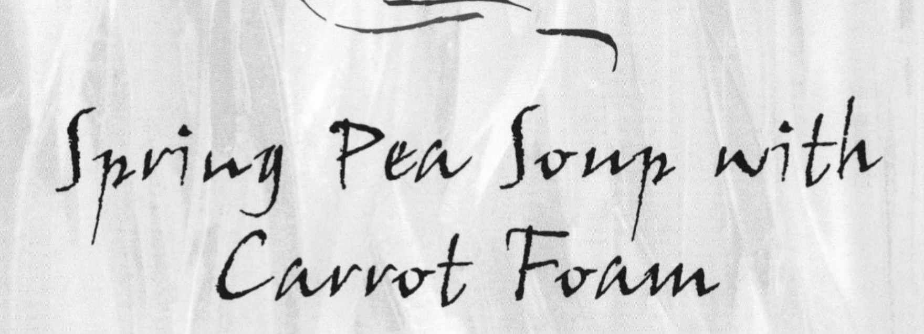

Spring Pea Soup with Carrot Foam

SOUP

4 cups Chicken Stock *(page 26)*
3 cups fresh green peas, shelled, with the shells reserved
1/4 cup heavy cream
2 tablespoons butter
3 tablespoons freshly grated Parmesan cheese
2 tablespoons chopped fresh mint
kosher salt and white pepper to taste

CARROT FOAM

1 cup carrot juice
2 tablespoons heavy cream
1/4 cup coconut milk
1 tablespoon butter

To prepare the soup, bring the Chicken Stock to a boil in a saucepan. Add the reserved pea shells. Remove from the heat and pour into a food processor or blender. Process until smooth; strain and return to the saucepan. Add the peas and cook for 4 to 5 minutes. Add the cream, butter, cheese and mint; season with kosher salt and white pepper. Blend just until smooth with a hand blender.

To prepare the carrot foam, combine the carrot juice, cream, coconut milk and butter in a saucepan. Bring to a boil. Blend until foamy with a hand blender.

To serve, ladle the soup into serving bowls. Top each serving with 2 tablespoons of carrot foam.

Makes 8 servings

Spring Veal Chops with Peas and Carrots and Vermouth Jus

VERMOUTH JUS
2 or 3 shallots, sliced
2 tablespoons butter
1 cup dry vermouth
4 cups Veal Stock ***(page 85)***
2 sprigs fresh thyme
1/2 teaspoon black peppercorns
pinch of caraway seeds

VEAL CHOPS WITH PEAS AND CARROTS
8 (14- to 16-ounce) veal chops
kosher salt and freshly ground black pepper to taste
3 tablespoons olive oil
32 baby carrots, peeled
1/2 cup green peas
1/2 cup fava beans, peeled
2 tablespoons olive oil
1 tablespoon butter
Parmesan Risotto ***(page 83)***

To prepare the vermouth jus, sauté the shallots in the butter in a large saucepan until tender, about 3 or 4 minutes. Deglaze the saucepan with the vermouth and cook until reduced by 1/2.

Add the Veal Stock, thyme, peppercorns and caraway seeds. Bring to a boil and cook until reduced to 2 cups. Strain and discard the solids.

To prepare the veal with peas and carrots, preheat the oven to 400 degrees. Season the veal chops with kosher salt and pepper. Heat 3 tablespoons olive oil in a sauté pan and add the veal chops. Sear over medium-high heat until well browned. Remove to a roasting pan and roast for 10 to 12 minutes, turning over once.

Blanch the carrots, peas and fava beans separately in boiling salted water in saucepans, cooking until each is tender. Shock each immediately in ice water to stop the cooking process and drain.

Heat 2 tablespoons olive oil in a sauté pan and add the peas and carrots. Sauté until tender. Season with kosher salt and pepper and add the butter.

To serve, spoon the Parmesan Risotto onto serving plates. Spoon the vegetable mixture beside the risotto. Place a veal chop on each plate, arranging the bone between the risotto and vegetables. Spoon the vermouth jus over the veal chop.

Makes 8 servings

Parmesan Risotto

1 quart water
5 shallots, chopped
2 tablespoons butter
2 cups uncooked arborio rice
3/4 cup white wine
kosher salt and freshly ground black pepper to taste
2 ounces Parmesan cheese, grated

Bring the water to a boil in a saucepan; reduce the heat and keep hot.

Sauté the shallots in the butter in a saucepan over medium heat for 2 to 3 minutes. Add the rice and stir until coated with butter. Sauté until heated through. Add the wine and cook until reduced by 1/2.

Add the hot water 1 cup at a time, cooking for 5 minutes or until the water is absorbed after each addition and stirring constantly. Season with kosher salt and pepper to taste. Add the cheese and mix well.

Makes 8 servings

Colorado Lamb Rack with Peruvian Potatoes and Spring Ratatouille

LAMB
4 (8-bone) lamb racks, frenched (see Note)
kosher salt and freshly ground black pepper to taste
3 tablespoons olive oil
Madeira Mirin Glaze ***(page 85)***

PERUVIAN POTATOES
10 large Peruvian purple potatoes
2 1/2 cups heavy cream
1/4 cup (1/2 stick) butter
kosher salt and freshly ground black pepper to taste

SPRING RATATOUILLE
2 tablespoons olive oil
1 medium onion, finely chopped
3 garlic cloves, minced
1 red bell pepper, finely chopped
1 eggplant, finely chopped
1 zucchini, finely chopped
1 yellow squash, finely chopped
1/2 cup roasted or sun-dried tomatoes
1 tablespoon capers
1/4 cup chopped fresh basil
1 1/2 teaspoons chopped fresh sage
kosher salt and freshly ground black pepper to taste

To prepare the lamb, preheat the oven to 400 degrees. Season the lamb racks with kosher salt and pepper. Heat the olive oil in a pan and add the lamb. Sear until well browned on all sides. Cover the bones with foil to prevent burning and roast the lamb for 10 to 12 minutes for medium, turning on all sides during roasting. Remove from the oven and keep warm.

To prepare the Peruvian potatoes, boil the potatoes in enough salted water to cover until tender, about 20 to 30 minutes. Remove and drain well. Peel and pass through a food mill or ricer. Heat the cream and butter together in a saucepan until hot. Add to the potatoes and stir until creamy and smooth. Season with kosher salt and pepper.

To prepare the spring ratatouille, heat the olive oil in a skillet and add the onion, garlic and bell pepper. Sauté until light brown, about 5 to 6 minutes. Add the eggplant and sauté for 3 to 4 minutes. Add the zucchini and squash and sauté for 2 to 3 minutes. Add the tomatoes, capers, basil and sage and season with kosher salt and pepper.

To serve, slice each lamb rack in half and place 4 lamb chops on each plate. Spoon the potatoes and ratatouille onto the plate. Spoon the Madiera-Mirin Glaze over the lamb and around the plate.

NOTE: Ask your butcher to prepare the lamb by frenching the bones.

Makes 8 servings

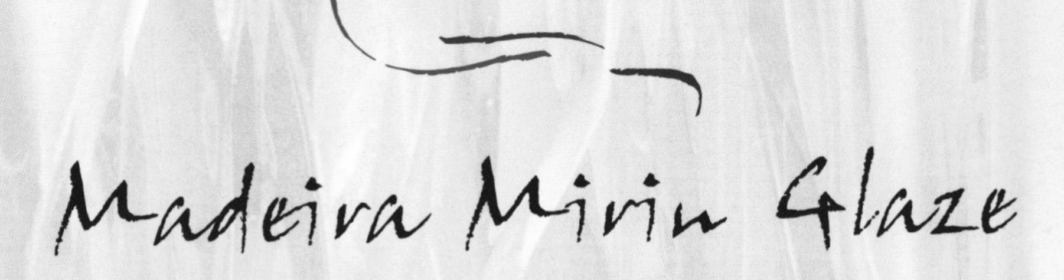

Madeira Mirin Glaze

2 cups madeira wine
1 cup mirin wine
4 cups Veal Stock *(below)* or beef stock
1/2 cup tamarind purée
1 star anise
3 shallots, chopped
1 sprig fresh thyme

Combine the madeira and mirin in a saucepan. Cook until reduced by 1/2. Add the Veal Stock, tamarind purée, star anise, shallots and thyme and simmer over medium heat for 1 hour or until reduced by 1/2. Strain and discard the solids.

Makes 1 1/2 cups

Veal Stock

5 pounds veal bones
1/2 cup vegetable oil or canola oil
3 ounces tomato paste
4 cups water
3 cups coarsely chopped carrots
3 medium onions, coarsely chopped
2 medium leeks, white and light green portions only, cleaned and coarsely chopped
4 sprigs fresh thyme
1 bay leaf

Preheat the oven to 450 degrees. Combine the veal bones and vegetable oil in a roasting pan. Roast until well browned, about 1 hour. Remove to a large stockpot.

Add the tomato paste to the roasting pan and cook on the stove top until caramelized, about 4 to 5 minutes. Deglaze the pan with 4 cups water, scraping all browned bits from roasting the bones. Cook until reduced by 1/2. Add to the stockpot with the bones.

Add the carrots, onions, leeks, thyme and bay leaf and add enough cold water to cover the bones by 2 inches. Bring to a boil, reduce the heat and simmer for 4 to 6 hours. Strain through a fine sieve.

Skim off any impurities from the remaining stock and pour into a saucepan. Cook over medium heat until reduced to 4 cups.

Makes 4 cups

Gulf Snapper with Lobster Tomato Marinara

Lobster Tomato Marinara
1 medium onion, finely chopped
2 garlic cloves, minced
1 tablespoon olive oil
1 cup Lobster Stock *(page 87)*
2 cups tomato juice
1/2 cup roasted tomatoes or sun-dried tomatoes
1/2 sprig fresh rosemary
1 sprig fresh thyme
kosher salt and pepper to taste
3 heirloom tomatoes, seeded and chopped

Vegetable Cassoulet
6 carrots, chopped
1/2 cup fava beans, peeled
1/2 cup green peas
1 turnip, peeled and chopped
2 tablespoons butter
3 medium shallots, minced
1 medium leek, white and light green portions only, chopped
1/2 cup chopped mushrooms
kosher salt and pepper to taste

Snapper
3 tablespoons vegetable oil
8 (8-ounce) snapper fillets
kosher salt and pepper to taste
2 cups Wild Mushroom Risotto *(page 87)*

To prepare the marinara sauce, sauté the onion and garlic in the olive oil for 3 to 4 minutes until tender. Add the next 5 ingredients. Season with salt and pepper. Cook for 10 to 15 minutes, or until the roasted tomatoes are tender. Add the heirloom tomatoes and cook for 5 to 8 minutes longer. Remove from the heat and discard the herbs. Process until smooth; keep warm.

To prepare the vegetable cassoulet, blanch the carrots, fava beans, peas and turnip in boiling water in a saucepan, then shock in ice water to stop the cooking process. Drain and set aside. Melt the butter in a sauté pan and add the shallots, leek and mushrooms. Sauté until tender, about 5 to 6 minutes. Add the carrots, fava beans, peas and turnip and season with kosher salt and pepper. Sauté over medium-high heat until cooked through. Keep warm.

To prepare the snapper, preheat the oven to 400 degrees. Heat the vegetable oil in an ovenproof skillet. Pat the snapper fillets dry and season with kosher salt and pepper. Sear skin side down in the oil until crisp. Turn the fillets and sear for 3 to 4 minutes longer. Bake for 3 to 4 minutes to finish.

To serve, spoon the Wild Mushroom Risotto onto serving plates. Top with the snapper and marinara sauce. Add the vegetable cassoulet.

Makes 8 servings

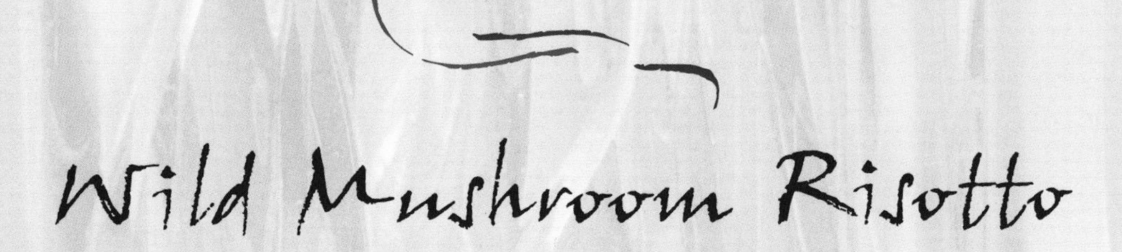

Wild Mushroom Risotto

4 cups water
5 shallots, chopped
2 tablespoons butter
2 cups uncooked arborio rice
3/4 cup white wine
kosher salt and pepper to taste
2 ounces (1/2 cup) grated Parmesan cheese
2 cups chopped and sautéed mixed wild mushrooms

Bring the water to a boil in a saucepan. Reduce the heat and keep hot. Sauté the shallots in the butter in a saucepan over medium heat for 2 to 3 minutes. Add the rice and stir until coated with butter. Sauté until heated through. Add the wine and cook until reduced by 1/2.

Add the hot water 1 cup at a time and cook for 5 minutes after each addition or until the water is absorbed, stirring constantly. Season with kosher salt and pepper to taste. Stir in the cheese and mushrooms.

Makes 8 servings

Lobster Stock

2 (1-pound) live lobsters
2 tablespoons vegetable oil
1 cup coarsely chopped onion
1 cup coarsely chopped carrots
1 cup cleaned and coarsely chopped leeks, white and light green portions
3 tablespoons tomato paste
1 cup white wine
4 cups water
3 sprigs fresh thyme
1/2 teaspoon whole black peppercorns

Boil the lobsters in enough water to cover in a saucepan for 8 minutes; remove and shock in ice water. Cool to room temperature, remove and reserve the shells. Reserve the lobster meat for another use.

Heat the vegetable oil in a large stockpot over medium-high heat. Add the lobster shells and cook for 4 to 5 minutes or until red in color. Add the onion, carrots and leeks and cook for 7 to 8 minutes. Add the tomato paste and cook for 2 to 3 minutes.

Stir in the wine and cook until reduced by 1/2. Add the water, thyme and peppercorns and bring to a boil. Reduce the heat to a simmer and cook for 40 minutes. Strain and return to the saucepan. Cook until reduced to 1 cup.

Makes 1 cup

Oysters Three Ways

Meyer Lemon Relish
1 Meyer lemon, thinly sliced
1 tablespoon kosher salt
2 tablespoons sugar
juice of 1 lemon
2 tablespoons rice wine vinegar
1 teaspoon chopped fresh chives
1 shallot, finely chopped
kosher salt and freshly ground black pepper to taste

48 oysters, such as Blue Point or other local variety, shucked

Cucumber Mignonette
1 English cucumber
1 shallot, chopped
1 tablespoon rice wine vinegar
2 tablespoons mirin wine
kosher salt and freshly ground black pepper to taste

Wasabi Granita
1/4 cup Japanese sake
1/4 cup mirin wine
1 cup water
2 teaspoons wasabi powder

To prepare the lemon relish, place the lemon slices in a bowl and sprinkle with with 1 tablespoon kosher salt and the sugar. Chill in the refrigerator for 24 to 48 hours. Rinse in a bowl of cold water and pat dry.

Chop the lemon finely. Combine with the lemon juice, vinegar, chives and shallot in a bowl and mix well. Season with kosher salt and pepper.

To prepare the cucumber mignonette, peel and purée the cucumber. Combine with the shallot, vinegar and mirin in a bowl. Season with kosher salt and pepper and mix well. Chill until serving time.

To prepare the wasabi granita, whisk the sake, mirin and water into the wasabi powder in a bowl. Strain into a shallow dish. Place in the freezer for 1 hour. Scrape the mixture with a fork to granulate. Freeze until firm and scrape again to make ice crystals.

To serve, place 6 oysters on each serving plate. Top 2 with Meyer lemon relish, 2 with cucumber mignonette and 2 with wasabi granita.

Makes 8 servings

Rabbit Confit with Goat Cheese Dumplings

Parmesan Broth
2 cups Chicken Stock *(page 26)*
1/2 cup (2 ounces) freshly grated Parmesan cheese

Rabbit Confit
front and back legs from 2 rabbits (see Note)
1 1/2 tablespoons kosher salt
2 1/2 tablespoons sugar
6 bay leaves
2 sprigs fresh thyme
6 cloves garlic, chopped
1 (1-inch) piece gingerroot, sliced
canola oil
loin pieces from 2 rabbits (see Note)
kosher salt and freshly ground black pepper to taste
2 tablespoons olive oil
1/2 cup green peas
1 tablespoon butter
Goat Cheese Dumplings *(page 91)*
1 teaspoon chopped fresh chives
1 teaspoon chopped fresh chervil
1 teaspoon chopped fresh tarragon

To prepare the Parmesan broth, bring the Chicken Stock to a boil in a saucepan. Whisk in the cheese quickly. Cook for 1 minute, whisking constantly. Strain through a fine mesh strainer. Store in the refrigerator.

To prepare the rabbit confit, place the rabbit legs in a baking pan. Combine the kosher salt and sugar and sprinkle over the legs. Place the bay leaves and thyme on top. Sprinkle with the garlic and gingerroot. Cover with plastic wrap and refrigerate for 12 hours or overnight.

Preheat the oven to 250 degrees. Remove the rabbit legs from the refrigerator; scrape off and discard the topping. Pat dry with paper towels to remove any fluid. Place in an ovenproof dish just large enough to hold the rabbit. Cover with canola oil and roast for 3 to 4 hours. Remove and let cool. Remove the meat from the bones and shred. Set aside.

Season the rabbit loin with kosher salt and pepper. Heat the olive oil in a large skillet. Add the rabbit loin and sear over high heat on both sides until golden brown. Add the Parmesan broth and peas. Add the butter and bring to a simmer. Reduce the heat to medium and cook 3 to 5 minutes. Add the shredded rabbit, Goat Cheese Dumplings and fresh herbs. Stir to combine and cook until heated through.

NOTE: Ask your butcher to cut the rabbit into pieces, separating the legs and loin.

Makes 8 servings

Goat Cheese Dumplings

1$^{1}/_{2}$ pounds goat cheese
1 egg, beaten
$^{1}/_{4}$ cup (1 ounce) freshly grated Parmesan cheese
1 teaspoon chopped fresh chives
1 teaspoon chopped fresh chervil
1 teaspoon chopped fresh tarragon
freshly ground black pepper to taste
$^{1}/_{2}$ cup (about) all-purpose flour
1 tablespoon kosher salt
2 tablespoons olive oil

Combine the goat cheese and egg in a mixing bowl; mix well. Add the Parmesan cheese, herbs and pepper. Mix to form a ball.

Dust some of the flour onto a clean surface. Place the goat cheese mixture on the surface and sprinkle with additional flour a little at a time, kneading until combined, about 4 or 5 times; dough should spring back at a light touch.

Bring water and the kosher salt to a boil in a large saucepan. Drop 1 teaspoon of the dough into the water as a test; the dumpling should hold together and float to the surface after 1 minute.

Cut the remaining dough into thirds. Roll each third into a long rope. Cut each rope into 1-inch pieces. Add to the water in batches and cook for 1 minute or until the dumplings float to the surface. Remove immediately to a bowl of ice water. Transfer with a slotted spoon to a bowl coated with the olive oil. Repeat until all the dumplings are cooked.

Makes 8 servings

Celebrity chef Todd English brings the flavors of Tuscany to Mohegan Sun. This 200-seat restaurant serves authentic regional Italian cuisine with an accent on freshness and quality. The menu features a variety of salads, appetizers, flatbreads, homemade pastas, and signature grilled and baked entrées.

Bibb Lettuce with a Shower of Roquefort Cheese

Tuscan Flatbread Fig Jam

The Tuscan Cut with Broccolini
Tuscan Potatoes

Kirsch-Braised Pork Shanks
Sweet Potato Polenta

Pan-Seared Sea Scallops

Chilean Sea Bass with Proscuitto-Wrapped Greens
and Tamari Jus

Herb Gnocchi

Tomato Confit Olive Confit

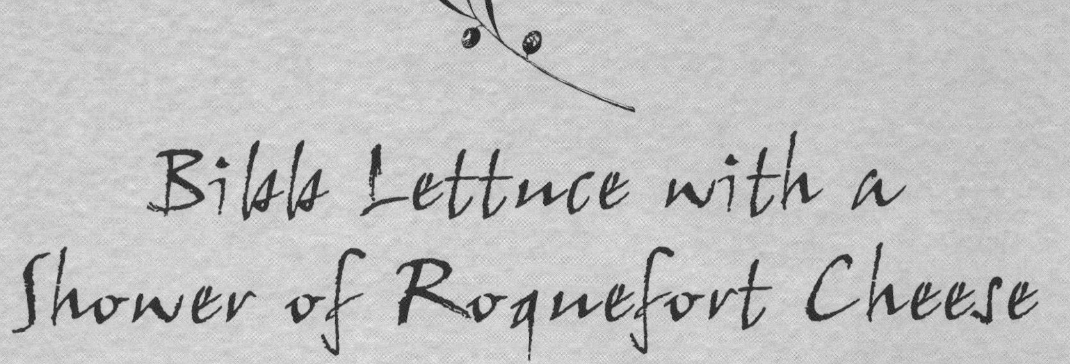

Bibb Lettuce with a Shower of Roquefort Cheese

2 tablespoons walnut oil
2/3 cup chopped walnuts
2 tablespoons fresh lemon juice
(about 1/2 lemon)
Splash of balsamic vinegar
2 heads Bibb lettuce, well washed,
dried, and torn into bite-size pieces
1/4 white onion, very thinly sliced
1 teaspoon kosher salt
1/2 teaspoon black pepper
1/2 cup shaved or crumbled
Roquefort cheese
(about 2 1/2 ounces)

Place a small skillet over medium-high heat and when it is hot, add the oil. Add the walnuts and cook until they are lightly toasted, about 3 minutes. Off the heat, add the lemon juice and vinegar.

In a large bowl, mix the lettuce, onion, salt and pepper.

Divide the lettuce among 4 plates and pour the hot dressing over it. Add the Roquefort cheese and serve immediately.

Makes 4 servings

NOTE: To achieve a “shower” of Roquefort cheese, first place the cheese in the freezer for at least 20 minutes. Put a chunk in a rotary cheese grater and grate onto the lettuce.

Tuscan Flatbread

1 cup balsamic vinegar
2 tablespoons sugar
Figs Pizza Dough crust *(page 95)*
1/4 cup semolina flour
1/4 cup olive oil with 1 tablespoon chopped fresh rosemary
1/3 cup Fig Jam *(below)*
5 or 6 slices fontina cheese
1/2 cup (2 ounces) crumbled Gorgonzola cheese
1 tablespoon chopped fresh rosemary
4 slices prosciutto
1/4 cup freshly grated Parmesan cheese

Combine the vinegar and sugar in a small saucepan. Cook until reduced by 2/3. Remove from the heat and cool. Preheat the oven to 500 degrees. Roll the Figs Pizza Dough into a 6×12-inch rectangle following the recipe directions and place on a baking sheet that has been dusted with the semolina flour. Brush with the rosemary oil.

Spread the Fig Jam over the dough. Layer the fontina cheese over the jam. Sprinkle the Gorgonzola cheese over the top. Sprinkle with the fresh rosemary. Bake until the cheese melts and crust if golden brown, about 7 minutes. Remove from oven and arrange the sliced proscuitto over the top. Garnish with the Parmesan cheese and drizzle with the balsamic reduction.

Makes 1 or 2 servings

Fig Jam

2 tablespoons olive oil
3/4 teaspoon chopped garlic
3/4 teaspoon chopped shallot
1 ounce fresh gingerroot, chopped
5 cups orange juice
1/2 cup Grand Marnier
1/4 cup sugar
1/4 cup brandy
1 pound dried figs, stems removed and sliced
3 sprigs fresh rosemary
1/2 cup water, as needed

Heat the olive oil in a large saucepan and add the garlic, shallot and gingerroot. Sauté until tender. Add the orange juice, Grand Marnier, sugar and brandy.

Bring to a boil and reduce the heat. Simmer for about 15 minutes. Add the figs and rosemary and simmer until the figs are tender, about 15 minutes longer. Remove from the heat, remove the rosemary sprigs and cool. Process in a food processor or blender and purée until smooth, adding the water if needed for the desired consistency.

Makes 1 1/2 to 2 cups

Figs Pizza Dough

1/4 cup whole-wheat flour
3 1/2 cups all-purpose flour, plus additional for rolling
2 teaspoons (1/4 ounce) fresh yeast
2 teaspoons kosher salt
2 teaspoons sugar
2 teaspoons olive oil
1 2/3 cups lukewarm water

Place the whole-wheat flour, all-purpose flour, yeast, salt and sugar in a mixer fitted with a dough hook. While the mixer is running, gradually add the oil and water. Knead on low speed until the dough is firm and smooth, about 10 minutes.

Divide the dough into four balls, about 7 1/2 ounces each. Line two cookie sheets with parchment paper. Place two balls on a sheet and cover with a damp towel. Let rise in a warm spot until doubled in bulk, about 2 hours.

To roll out the dough: Dab your fingers in flour and then place 1 ball on a generously floured surface and press down in the center with the tips of your fingers, spreading the dough with your hand. When the dough has doubled in width, use a floured rolling pin and roll out until it is very thin, like flatbread. The outer border should be a little thicker than the inner circle. Pick the dough up with a spatula or the back of a knife, allowing it to fold up almost like an umbrella and transfer it to a paddle. Do not worry that the pizza is not round, you are looking for an 8- to 10-inch shape, a cross between an oval and a rectangle. If you get a hole, simply pinch the edges back together. Repeat with the remaining balls.

Makes four 8- to 10-inch pizzas
Serves 1 to 2 people per pizza

The Tuscan Cut with Broccolini and Red Wine Reduction

1 bottle cabernet wine
salt to taste
2 pounds broccolini
1 to 3 tablespoons olive oil
4 (16- to 22-ounce) porterhouse steaks
kosher salt and freshly ground black pepper to taste
6 tablespoons (3/4 stick) unsalted butter
1/2 cup julienned shiitake mushroom caps
Tuscan Potatoes ***(page 97)***

Cook the wine in a medium saucepan over low to medium heat until reduced to about 1/4 of the original volume; do not boil. Let stand for 1 hour.

Bring a large saucepot of salted water to a boil. Trim the stems of the broccolini. Cook the trimmed broccolini in the boiling water until tender; do not overcook. Plunge immediately into ice water to stop the cooking process and keep the bright green color. Set aside.

Preheat the broiler. Heat a large sauté pan over medium-high heat and add the olive oil. Season both sides of each steak with kosher salt and pepper. Add to the sauté pan and sear on both sides until brown. Remove to a broiler pan and broil until done to taste.

Heat a small sauté pan over medium heat. Add 1 tablespoon of the butter and heat until almost golden brown. Add the mushrooms and sauté until golden brown and fully cooked. Season with kosher salt and pepper.

Melt 2 tablespoons of the butter in a sauté pan and add the broccolini. Sauté just to serving temperature.

Reheat the red wine reduction until warm. Whisk in up to 3 tablespoons of the remaining butter to enrich the sauce.

To serve, spoon the Tuscan Potatoes onto the center of each serving plate. Add a couple of spears of broccolini to the top of the potatoes. Place the steaks on top, leaving some of the tips of the broccolini exposed. Drizzle the steaks with the red wine reduction. Garnish with the shiitake mushrooms.

Makes 4 servings

Tuscan Potatoes

5 or 6 large Yukon Gold potatoes
1 tablespoon olive oil
kosher salt and freshly ground black pepper to taste
1 pound pancetta or bacon, sliced about 1/4 inch thick and chopped
1 yellow or white onion, julienned
1 tablespoon unsalted butter
1 teaspoon sugar
2 tablespoons water
2 tablespoons unsalted butter
1/4 cup sour cream

Preheat the oven to 350 degrees. Cut the unpeeled potatoes into wedges. Toss with the olive oil in a bowl and season with kosher salt and pepper. Place on a baking sheet or in a baking dish and roast for about 45 minutes or until the potatoes are cooked through and golden brown.

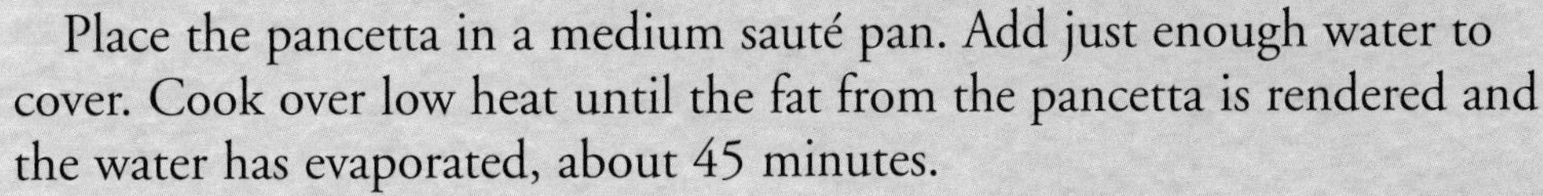

Place the pancetta in a medium sauté pan. Add just enough water to cover. Cook over low heat until the fat from the pancetta is rendered and the water has evaporated, about 45 minutes.

Combine the onion, 1 tablespoon butter, sugar and 2 tablespoons water in a small saucepan. Cook over medium heat until the onion is tender and translucent and the liquid has evaporated, about 20 minutes. Cool and set aside.

Heat a large sauté pan. Add 2 tablespoons butter, the sautéed onion and the rendered pancetta. Cook until heated through. Add the roasted potatoes and heat to serving temperature. Remove from the heat and fold in the sour cream; do not return to the heat after adding the sour cream.

NOTE: Rendering is the process of removing fat from the meat by a slow heat process.

Makes 4 servings

Kirsch-Braised Pork Shanks

4 pork shanks, tied with twine
kosher salt and freshly ground black pepper to taste
1 cup all-purpose flour
1/2 cup olive oil
10 slices bacon, chopped
4 cloves garlic, crushed
1 cup chopped onion
1 1/2 cups chopped carrots
1 cup chopped fennel
1 cup cleaned and chopped leeks, white and light green parts only
3 cups cherry brandy, such as Kirsch
4 quarts Chicken Stock *(page 26)*
5 sprigs fresh rosemary
5 sprigs fresh tarragon
grated zest of 1 orange
5 black peppercorns
2 bay leaves
Sweet Potato Polenta *(below)*

Season the pork shanks with kosher salt and pepper and coat with the flour. Heat the olive oil in a cast-iron skillet and sear each shank until brown on all sides. Transfer to a large roasting pan.

Cook the bacon in a large stockpot until the fat is rendered. Add the garlic, onion, carrots, fennel and leeks. Cook until light brown, about 15 minutes. Deglaze with the cherry brandy and cook until heated through. Add the Chicken Stock, rosemary, tarragon, orange zest, peppercorns, bay leaves and kosher salt to taste. Simmer for about 30 minutes. Spoon over the pork shanks.

Preheat the oven to 300 degrees. Roast the pork and vegetables, covered, for 5 to 6 hours, or until the pork is tender. Spoon the Polenta onto plates. Top with the pork shanks and cooking juices.

Makes 4 servings

Sweet Potato Polenta

3 sweet potatoes
1/4 cup honey
3/4 cup milk
1/2 cup (1 stick) unsalted butter
4 cups cooked polenta
kosher salt and freshly ground black pepper to taste

Preheat the oven to 375 degrees. Roast the sweet potatoes for 30 to 35 minutes. Cool and peel the potatoes. Place in a bowl and mash with a fork.

Heat the honey in a medium saucepan until caramelized. Combine with the sweet potatoes in a large saucepan and mix well. Add the milk and butter and bring to a simmer. Add the polenta and mix well. Season with kosher salt and pepper.

Makes 4 servings

Pan-Seared Sea Scallops

2 cups uncooked risotto
2 tablespoons fresh lemon juice
2 tablespoons unsalted butter
1 cup seasonal citrus juice, such as orange juice or pineapple juice
4 tablespoons (1/2 stick) unsalted butter, chilled
16 large sea scallops
kosher salt and freshly ground black pepper to taste
2 tablespoons olive oil
1/4 cup tangerine honey
2 tablespoons pine nuts, toasted
2 tablespoons grated lemon zest

Prepare the risotto according to the package directions. Fold the lemon juice and 2 tablespoons butter into the cooked risotto.

Bring the citrus juice to a simmer in a small saucepan and cook until reduced to 1/3. Whisk in 4 tablespoons cold butter gradually to form a sauce. Keep warm away from direct heat.

Season the scallops with kosher salt and pepper. Heat the olive oil in a sauté pan and add the scallops. Sear the scallops until golden brown on each side, about 2 to 3 minutes per side.

Place the risotto in a serving dish. Arrange the seared scallops on top and drizzle with the honey. Drizzle the citrus butter sauce around the risotto and top with the toasted pine nuts and lemon zest.

Makes 4 servings

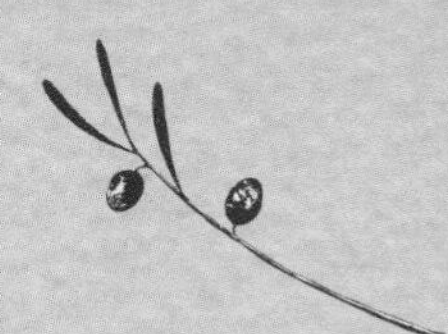

Chilean Sea Bass with Prosciutto-Wrapped Greens and Tamari Jus

1 bunch baby carrots, about 8 to 10 carrots
1 tablespoon olive oil
kosher salt and freshly ground black pepper to taste
1 tablespoon olive oil
4 (8-ounce) portions Chilean sea bass
2 cups Demi Glace ***(page 101)***
1/2 cup tamari soy sauce
4 tablespoons (1/2 stick) butter
4 cups mesclun greens
1 tablespoon red wine vinegar
1/4 cup olive oil
12 slices prosciutto

Preheat the oven to 350 degrees. Clean carrots and toss with 1 tablespoon olive oil, kosher salt and pepper in a roasting pan. Roast until tender, about 25 minutes.

Heat 1 tablespoon olive oil in an ovenproof sauté pan over medium-high heat. Season the bass with kosher salt and pepper. Add to the sauté pan and sear until each side is golden brown. Transfer to the oven and bake until cooked through, about 8 to 10 minutes. Bring the Demi Glace to a simmer in a saucepan and cook until reduced by 1/2. Reduce the heat and add the tamari soy sauce, mixing well. Add 4 tablespoons butter gradually and cook to sauce consistency, stirring constantly. Cover.

Toss the mesclun greens with the vinegar and 1/4 cup olive oil in a bowl. Spoon the mesclun mixture onto the prosciutto and roll to enclose the greens. Place 3 rolls on each of 4 plates. Place the bass on top of the prosciutto-wrapped greens. Drizzle with the tamari jus and top with the cooked carrots to serve.

Makes 4 servings

Demi Glace

3 tablespoons olive oil
1/2 cup chopped onion
1/2 cup chopped carrot
1/4 cup chopped celery
4 cups low-sodium beef broth

Heat the olive oil in a large stockpot. Add the onion, carrot and celery and cook until caramelized and lightly browned. Add the beef broth and simmer over medium heat until reduced to a sauce consistency, about 45 minutes. Strain and discard the vegetables.

Makes 1 to 1 1/2 cups

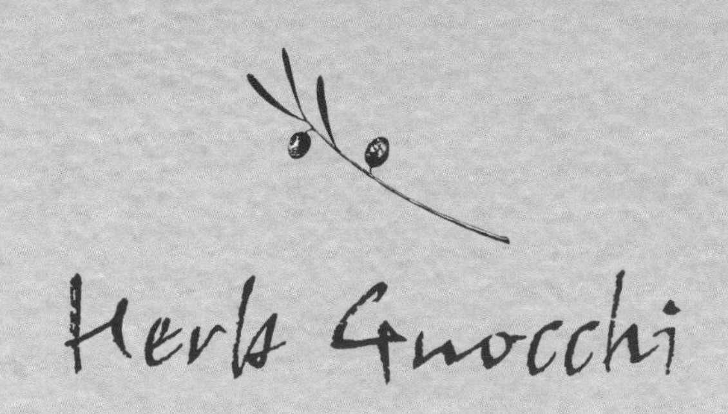

Herb Gnocchi

GNOCCHI
10 Yukon Gold potatoes
kosher salt and freshly ground black pepper to taste
16 ounces ricotta cheese
1/3 cup chopped fresh basil
1/3 cup chopped fresh sage
2 tablespoons chopped fresh thyme
2 large eggs
2/3 cup grated Parmesan cheese
4 cups semolina flour
2 cups all-purpose flour

GNOCCHI SAUCE
2 tablespoons olive oil
1 teaspoon chopped garlic
1 teaspoon chopped shallots
2 tablespoons chopped fresh basil
2 tablespoons chopped fresh sage
1/2 cup white wine
2 tablespoons Tomato Confit ***(page 103)***
1 tablespoon Olive Confit ***(page 103)***
2 to 4 tablespoons unsalted butter
kosher salt to taste
grated Parmesan cheese

To prepare the gnocchi, preheat the oven to 350 degrees. Bake the potatoes for 1 hour; cool and peel the potatoes. Pass through a food mill or potato ricer. Season with kosher salt and pepper.

Combine the ricotta cheese, basil, sage, thyme and eggs in a large bowl. Add the processed potatoes and mix well. Mix in the Parmesan cheese. Fold in the semolina flour 1/3 cup at a time, alternating with small amounts of the all-purpose flour until the potato mixture starts to form a dough consistency and springs back slowly from a light touch.

Cut the dough into 4 portions and roll into 3/4-inch diameter logs on a floured surface. Cut into 3/4-inch pieces. Dust with additional semolina flour and refrigerate until ready to use.

To prepare the sauce, heat the olive oil in a saucepan and add the garlic and shallots. Sauté until translucent but not brown. Add the basil and sage and mix well. Add the wine and cook until reduced by 1/3.

Stir in the Tomato Confit and the Olive Confit. Cook until reduced by 1/3. Stir in the butter and cook until reduced to a sauce consistency. Keep warm over low heat.

Bring a saucepan of water to a boil and add the gnocchi and kosher salt. Cook until the gnocchi are tender, about 4 to 5 minutes, taking care not to overcook. Drain and add to the sauce. Toss well and serve with grated Parmesan cheese.

Makes 4 servings

Tomato Confit

2 pints cherry tomatoes
4 sprigs fresh thyme
1/2 cup olive oil
kosher salt and freshly ground black pepper to taste

Cut the cherry tomatoes into halves. Remove the thyme leaves from stems. Toss the tomatoes, thyme leaves and olive oil together in a bowl. Season with kosher salt and pepper.

Preheat the oven to 350 degrees. Spread the tomato mixture on a baking sheet and roast until the tomatoes are cooked through, about 2 hours.

Makes 2 cups

Olive Confit

2 cups oil-cured kalamata olives
2 tablespoons olive oil

Preheat the oven to 350 degrees.

Toss the olives with the olive oil in a bowl, coating well. Spread on a baking sheet and roast until olives are tender, about 10 to 15 minutes.

Makes 2 cups

If it is Italian fare that you crave, Pompeii and Caesar is just the spot for you. Escape to a romantic grotto rich in velvety shades of red and blue, and experience Italian cuisine as it is meant to be. The name of this restaurant honors both Mohegan and Roman history, for the grandson and great grandson of the legendary Mohegan leader Uncas were named Caesar and Pompeii, reflecting Uncas' recommendation that his people emulate those powerful Roman leaders.

Minestrone

Caesar Salad

Focaccia with Roasted Garlic Fondue

Veal Milanese

Bisteca de Manzo

Chicken Ripieno

Calamari Fritti

Linguini with White Clam Sauce

Pappardelle

Minestrone

1 medium onion, chopped
1 carrot, chopped
2 ribs celery, chopped
1 tablespoon olive oil
3/4 cup white wine
8 leaves fresh basil
3 sprigs fresh thyme
3 sprigs fresh rosemary
8 cups water
2 small potatoes, peeled and chopped
1 zucchini, chopped
2 tablespoons pesto

Sweat the onion, carrot and celery in the olive oil in a saucepan until the onions are translucent. Add the white wine and cook until reduced by 1/2.

Tie the basil, thyme and rosemary in a bundle with butcher's twine to make a bouquet garni. Add to the vegetables. Add the water and bring to a boil. Add the potatoes and cook until tender, about 5 minutes. Remove from the heat and add the zucchini.

Place 3 ladles of the soup mixture into a blender and add the pesto; process until smooth. Return the puréed mixture to the soup and stir to mix well. Heat to serving temperature.

Makes 8 servings

Caesar Salad

Croutons
4 cups cubed day-old bread
1/4 cup olive oil
1 clove garlic, minced
1 tablespoon dried oregano
1 tablespoon grated Parmesan cheese

Caesar Dressing
1 teaspoon chopped garlic
1 egg
1/2 cup (2 ounces) grated Parmesan cheese, or to taste
2 tablespoons red wine vinegar
1 teaspoon Dijon mustard
1/2 ounce anchovy fillets
freshly ground black pepper to taste
juice of 1 lemon
3/4 cup vegetable oil
3/4 cup olive oil

Salad
8 romaine lettuce hearts
3/4 cup (3 ounces) grated shaved Parmesan cheese
1/2 cup (2 ounces) shaved Parmesan cheese

To prepare the croutons, preheat the oven to 350 degrees. Toss the bread cubes with the olive oil, garlic, oregano and cheese. Spread the seasoned croutons on a baking sheet and bake until golden brown, about 3 to 4 minutes.

To prepare the dressing, combine the garlic, egg, cheese, vinegar, mustard, anchovy fillets, pepper and lemon juice in a food processor and process until smooth, about 1 minute.

Add the vegetable oil and olive oil gradually, processing constantly to form an emulsion. Add additional cheese, if desired.

To prepare the salad, rinse the romaine lettuce to remove any sand and tear into bite-size pieces. Combine with the dressing, grated cheese and croutons. Spoon into 8 salad bowls and top with the shaved cheese.

Makes 8 servings

Focaccia with Roasted Garlic Fondue

FOCACCIA
2 tablespoons active dry yeast
4 cups warm water
5 to 6 cups all-purpose flour
1 teaspoon salt
2 teaspoons freshly ground black pepper
2 tablespoons chopped fresh rosemary
1 cup (4 ounces) grated Parmesan cheese
6 tablespoons olive oil
kosher salt to taste

ROASTED GARLIC FONDUE
8 cloves Roasted Garlic (see Note, *page 77*)
2 cups cream
1/2 cup (2 ounces) finely chopped fontina cheese

To prepare the focaccia, dissolve the yeast in 1/2 cup of the water and let stand for 10 minutes until bubbly.

Combine the yeast mixture with 5 cups of the flour, the salt, pepper, rosemary and Parmesan cheese in a bowl. Add enough of the remaining warm water to make a sticky dough, mixing well with the hands and adding the additional flour as needed to keep the dough workable; you may not need all of the water. Place in an oiled bowl, turning to coat the surface. Cover with plastic wrap and let rise until doubled, about 1 1/2 hours.

Preheat the oven to 375 degrees. Punch down the dough and stretch over an oiled 9×11-inch baking sheet, or larger for a thinner, crispier focaccia. Dimple the surface with the fingers; drizzle with the olive oil and sprinkle with kosher salt. Bake until golden brown, about 25 minutes; cool and slice.

To prepare the fondue, mash the Roasted Garlic. Combine with the cream and fontina cheese in a sauté pan. Cook until the cream reduces and the sauce is thickened to the desired consistency.

Makes 8 servings

Veal Milanese

12 medium eggs
1/2 cup milk
4 cups all-purpose flour
5 cups bread crumbs
1/2 cup (2 ounces) grated Parmesan cheese
3 ounces garlic powder
3 ounces dried oregano
2 ounces dried thyme
kosher salt and pepper to taste
8 veal chops, pounded thin
olive oil for sautéing
1 clove garlic, chopped
2 tablespoons olive oil
2 pounds capellini, cooked al dente
6 tablespoons (3/4 stick) butter
3 ounces arugula, chiffonade
1 plum tomato, finely chopped
4 lemons, cut into halves

Whisk the eggs and milk together in a bowl. Place the flour in a shallow bowl or pie pan. Combine the bread crumbs, cheese, garlic powder, oregano, thyme, kosher salt and pepper in a third bowl. Coat the veal chops with the flour, then dip into the egg wash and finally into the seasoned bread crumbs, pressing to coat well. Sauté in 1/4-inch of olive oil in a sauté pan until golden brown on both sides. Set aside.

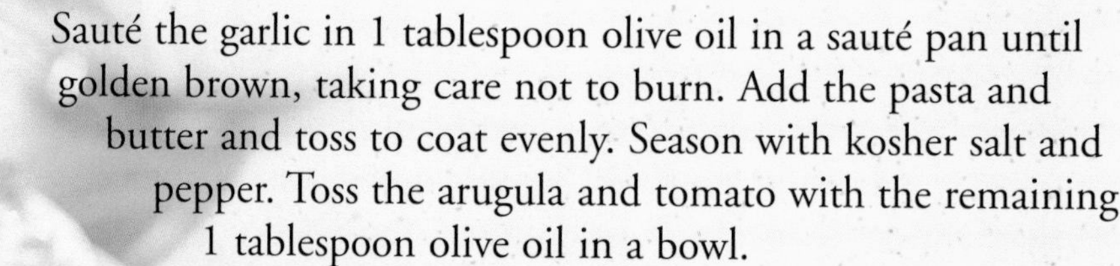

Sauté the garlic in 1 tablespoon olive oil in a sauté pan until golden brown, taking care not to burn. Add the pasta and butter and toss to coat evenly. Season with kosher salt and pepper. Toss the arugula and tomato with the remaining 1 tablespoon olive oil in a bowl.

To serve, spoon the pasta onto the side of each serving plate. Add the veal chops, placing the bone over the pasta. Top with the arugula and tomato mixture. Serve with a lemon half.

Makes 8 servings

Bisteca di Manzo

24 baby carrots
kosher salt to taste
1 pound broccoli rabe
24 small new potatoes
2 tablespoons olive oil
freshly ground black pepper to taste
8 (12-ounce) beef strip steaks
1 cup marsala wine
4 roasted red bell peppers, julienned
4 roasted yellow bell peppers, julienned
1/2 teaspoon chopped garlic
1/4 cup (1/2 stick) butter

Blanch the carrots in boiling salted water in a saucepan for 4 minutes; drain and place in ice water to stop the cooking process. Blanch the broccoli rabe in salted boiling water in a saucepan for 3 minutes, then shock in ice water. Blanch the potatoes in boiling water in a saucepan for 5 minutes, then shock in ice water.

Preheat the oven to 400 degrees. Toss the potatoes in the olive oil and season with kosher salt and pepper. Spread in a roasting pan and roast until fork tender, about 5 minutes.

Season the steaks and grill until done to taste; keep warm.

Combine the marsala, julienned peppers and half the garlic in a saucepan. Cook until reduced by 1/4. Add half the butter and cook until the sauce thickens.

Combine the carrots and broccoli rabe with the remaining garlic and butter in a saucepan and heat to serving temperature. Season with kosher salt and pepper.

To serve, spoon the vegetables and potatoes onto serving plates. Place the steaks over the potatoes and top with the wine sauce.

Makes 8 servings

Chicken Ripieno

CHICKEN
8 ounces asparagus
kosher salt to taste
24 baby carrots
16 ounces broccoli rabe
16 red potatoes
2 tablespoons olive oil
freshly ground black pepper to taste
8 (8-ounce) chicken breasts
3 ounces cooked ham, thinly sliced
2 ounces roasted red pepper strips
16 ounces fontina cheese, cut into thin 3-inch strips
1/2 cup (1 stick) butter
2 tablespoons each olive oil and butter

THYME CREAM SAUCE
2 bunches thyme
6 tablespoons olive oil
2 shallots, thinly sliced
2 cloves garlic, chopped
1/2 cup white wine
1 cup Chicken Stock ***(page 26)***
3 cups heavy cream
kosher salt and white pepper to taste
1/2 cup (1 stick) butter, as needed

To prepare the chicken, preheat the oven to 400 degrees. Blanch the asparagus in salted water in a saucepan. Plunge into ice water to stop the cooking process. Blanch the baby carrots and broccoli rabe in salted water in a saucepan and shock in ice water.

Blanch the potatoes in boiling salted water in a saucepan; cool and cut into quarters. Toss the potatoes with 2 tablespoons olive oil and season with kosher salt and pepper. Roast until golden brown.

Pound the chicken as thin as possible. Layer the ham, asparagus, roasted red pepper strips and cheese on the chicken. Fold the chicken to enclose the filling and roll into roulades. Melt 1/2 cup butter in a hot ovenproof sauté pan and add the chicken. Sauté until brown on both sides. Place in the oven and bake until cooked through, about 15 minutes.

Sauté the carrots and broccoli rabe in a sauté pan with 2 tablespoons butter and 2 tablespoons olive oil. Season with kosher salt and pepper.

To prepare the cream sauce, remove the thyme leaves from the stems and chop. Heat the olive oil in a saucepan and add the chopped thyme, shallots and garlic. Cook until the garlic is translucent, taking care not to burn. Add the white wine and cook until the liquid evaporates. Add the Chicken Stock, cream, kosher salt and white pepper and cook until the sauce begins to thicken, stirring constantly. Add enough butter gradually to give the desired consistency, stirring constantly.

To serve, spoon the carrots, broccoli and roasted potatoes onto serving plates. Slice the chicken and arrange across the vegetables. Top with the cream sauce.

Makes 8 servings

Calamari Fritti

$2^{1}/2$ pounds fresh calamari, cut into rings
6 cups all-purpose flour
1 ounce garlic powder
3 ounces paprika
2 tablespoons onion powder
kosher salt to taste
4 quarts vegetable oil
2 cups pepperoncini, cut into rings
1 tablespoon chopped fresh parsley
$^{1}/4$ teaspoon red pepper flakes
$^{1}/4$ teaspoon chopped garlic
2 cups Marinara Sauce ***(page 71)***
4 lemons, cut into halves

Rinse the calamari under cold water and drain well. Mix the flour with the garlic powder, paprika, onion powder and kosher salt in a large bowl. Coat the calamari with the seasoned flour, shaking off the excess.

Heat the vegetable oil to 350 degrees. Deep-fry the calamari in batches until golden brown, about 1 to 2 minutes. Remove from the oil with a slotted spoon and drain on paper towels. Toss with the pepperoncini, parsley and kosher salt in a bowl.

Add the red pepper flakes and chopped garlic to the Marinara Sauce in a saucepan. Heat to serving temperature.

Spoon the calamari into serving bowls and serve with a side of spicy Marinara Sauce and a lemon half.

Makes 8 servings

Linguini with White Clam Sauce

1 cup (2 sticks) butter
8 cloves garlic, chopped
1 pinch red pepper flakes
40 littleneck clams in shells
1 pound clam meat, chopped
2 tablespoons chopped fresh rosemary
2 cups white wine
1 cup olive oil
kosher salt to taste
3 pounds uncooked linguini
1/2 cup chopped fresh parsley for garnish

Melt the butter and cook until foamy in a large heavy saucepan over medium heat. Reduce the heat to medium-low and add the garlic. Sauté until translucent, stirring frequently. Add the red pepper flakes, clams, clam meat, rosemary, wine and olive oil. Cover the pan tightly and simmer until the clams in shells just open. Remove and discard any clams that do not open. Remove from the heat and keep warm.

Bring water to a boil in a large saucepan over high heat. Add the pasta and kosher salt and cook until the linguini is al dente, using the package directions. Drain the pasta well. Toss the pasta with the sauce and spoon into serving bowls. Garnish with clam shells and the parsley.

Makes 8 servings

Pappardelle

2 cloves garlic, chopped
1/4 cup olive oil
4 cups chopped tomatoes
1/2 bunch fresh basil, chiffonade
kosher salt and freshly ground black pepper to taste
1/2 cup white wine
5 cups Marinara Sauce *(page 71)*
1/2 cup cream
1 cup (4 ounces) shredded mozzarella cheese
3 pounds Fresh Pappardelle, cooked *(below)*
3 cups (12 ounces) cubed fresh mozzarella cheese

Sauté the garlic in the olive oil in a large sauté pan until golden brown, taking care not to burn. Add the tomatoes, basil, kosher salt and pepper and cook until the liquid has evaporated. Add the white wine and cook until reduced by 1/2.

Add the Marinara Sauce and cook until the sauce thickens. Stir in the cream and shredded mozzarella cheese. Add the pasta and toss to coat well. Spoon into serving bowls and sprinkle with the cubed mozzarella cheese.

NOTE: You can substitute dried pasta for the fresh pappardelle and cook using the package directions.

Makes 8 servings

Fresh Pappardelle

2 pounds all-purpose flour
6 whole eggs
3 egg yolks
1/4 cup olive oil
1 tablespoon salt

Combine the flour, eggs, egg yolks, olive oil and 1 tablespoon salt in a mixer fitted with a dough hook. Mix to form a smooth dough that does not stick to the hands. Let dough rest for at least 1 hour before rolling out.

Roll the dough paper thin and cut into 1×6-inch strips; sprinkle with additional flour. Cook the pasta strips in salted boiling water in a stockpot for 5 minutes. Drain well.

Makes 3 pounds

Low ceilings of intricately-cut Asian design create an intimate setting for a special dinner in the Bamboo Forest. There you can sample traditional and new dishes from the far East, including Thailand, Malaysia, and Vietnam. Or enjoy an evening with fine tea and a tantalizing selection of thirteen Dim Sum items.

Hot-and-Sour Soup

Crispy Tangerine Beef

Singapore Chicken and Beef Satay

Kung Pao Chicken

Moo Shu Pork

Pad Thai

Emperor-Style Soft-Shell Crabs

Grand Marnier Prawns

Jade Sea Scallops

Asian Eggplant with Garlic Sauce

Curry Fried Rice

Hot-and-Sour Soup

8 cups Chicken Stock *(page 26)*
10 ounces pork, cut into strips
10 ounces tofu, cut into strips
2 ounces wood ear mushrooms
6 ounces golden mushrooms
4 ounces bamboo strips
2 tablespoons salt
white pepper to taste
1/4 cup white vinegar
2 ounces chicken powder
1/4 cup mushroom soy sauce
2 tablespoons cornstarch
2 tablespoons water
4 eggs, beaten
1 tablespoon sesame oil

Combine the Chicken Stock, pork, tofu, mushrooms, bamboo strips, salt, pepper, vinegar, chicken powder and soy sauce in a large saucepan. Bring to a boil, reduce the heat and cook for 10 minutes. Adjust the seasonings if necessary.

Whisk the cornstarch and water together in a cup to make a slurry. Add the slurry slowly to the soup and cook until the soup thickens, about 1 to 2 minutes, stirring constantly. Remove from the heat.

Whisk in the beaten eggs gradually. Add the sesame oil and ladle into soup bowls.

Makes 8 servings

Crispy Tangerine Beef

5 pounds beef flank steak, cut into strips
8 eggs, beaten
1 cup cornstarch
vegetable oil for deep-frying
1/4 cup vegetable oil
1 1/2 tablespoons grated orange zest
1 1/2 tablespoons dry chile pepper
5 cups Chicken Stock *(page 26)*
3 tablespoons mushroom soy sauce
1/4 cup light soy sauce
1/2 cup sugar
1 1/2 tablespoons vinegar
5 tablespoons cornstarch
5 tablespoons water
4 ounces broccoli, blanched

Dip the beef in the eggs and coat with 1 cup cornstarch. Deep-fry in vegetable oil.

Heat 1/4 cup vegetable oil in a wok. Add the orange zest and chile pepper and stir-fry. Add the Chicken Stock, soy sauces, sugar and vinegar and mix well.

Blend 5 tablespoons cornstarch with the water to form a slurry. Add to the wok and cook until thickened, stirring constantly. Add the beef and mix well. Cook until heated through. Top with the broccoli.

Makes 8 servings

竹

Singapore Chicken and Beef Satay

1/4 cup vegetable oil
2 tablespoons white wine
1 tablespoon hoisin sauce
1 teaspoon soy sauce
1 tablespoon sugar
1 tablespoon oyster sauce
1 tablespoon chicken powder
2 pounds chicken tenders, cut into 16 long slices
2 pounds beef flank steak, cut into 16 long slices
1/4 cup coconut milk
1 cup peanut butter
sliced tomatoes, scallions and parsley for garnish

Combine the vegetable oil, wine, hoisin sauce, soy sauce, sugar, oyster sauce and chicken powder in a bowl. Add the chicken and beef and mix to coat well. Marinate for 30 minutes.

Soak 32 bamboo skewers in water for 30 minutes. Drain the chicken and beef and thread onto the skewers. Grill until cooked through.

Mix the coconut milk and peanut butter in a bowl. Place 2 chicken and 2 beef skewers on each serving plate. Serve with the peanut butter sauce and garnish with tomatoes, scallions and chopped parsley.

Makes 8 servings

Kung Pao Chicken

3 pounds boneless chicken breast, chopped
vegetable oil for deep-frying
2 green bell peppers, sliced
2 red bell peppers, sliced
1 (16-ounce) can sliced water chestnuts
1 rib celery, chopped
1/4 cup vegetable oil
2 tablespoons dry red chile pepper
2 cups kung pao sauce
2 tablespoons cornstarch
2 tablespoons water
10 ounces peanuts for garnish

Deep-fry the chicken in heated vegetable oil until cooked through, about 6 to 8 minutes. Remove to paper towels to drain.

Blanch the bell peppers, water chestnuts and celery in boiling water in a saucepan. Plunge into ice water to stop the cooking process.

Heat 1/4 cup vegetable oil in a wok and stir-fry the chile pepper. Add the chicken, blanched vegetables and kung pao sauce. Whisk the cornstarch and water together to form a slurry. Add to the wok and cook until thickened and heated through, stirring constantly. Garnish with the peanuts.

Makes 8 servings

Moo Shu Pork

4 tablespoons vegetable oil
1 pound pork, cut into strips
8 eggs, beaten
1 1/2 tablespoons chopped garlic
1 head cabbage, shredded
4 ounces wood ear mushrooms
4 ounces bamboo shoot strips
3 tablespoons chopped scallions
1/2 cup hoisin sauce
1 1/2 tablespoons mushroom soy sauce
1 tablespoon salt
1/4 cup sugar
1 1/2 tablespoons chicken powder
1 1/2 tablespoons sesame oil
1 package moo shu pancakes

Heat 2 tablespoons of the vegetable oil in a wok and stir-fry the pork and eggs until the pork is cooked through and the eggs are set. Remove to a separate plate.

Heat the remaining 2 tablespoons vegetable oil in the wok. Add the garlic, cabbage, mushrooms, bamboo shoots and scallions and stir-fry until tender. Add the hoisin sauce, soy sauce, salt, sugar and chicken powder. Stir-fry to blend the flavors. Add the pork and eggs to the mixture. Stir in the sesame oil. Serve with warmed moo shu pancakes.

NOTE: Moo shu pancakes are available at Asian markets or in the Asian section of your supermarket.

Makes 8 servings

Pad Thai

1/4 cup vegetable oil
4 eggs, beaten
3 pounds Thai noodles, cooked
12 ounces chicken tenders, cooked and chopped
12 ounces baby shrimp, cooked
4 ounces dry bean curd, cut into strips
2 ounces bean sprouts
2 scallions, chopped
6 tablespoons fish sauce
5 ounces sugar
4 ounces peanuts, crushed
1 red bell pepper, thinly sliced

Heat the the vegetable oil in a wok and stir-fry the eggs until done. Add the noodles, chicken, shrimp, bean curd, bean sprouts and scallions and stir-fry until heated through. Add the fish sauce and sugar and stir-fry quickly to heat through.

Spoon onto serving plates and top with crushed peanuts and red bell pepper slices.

Makes 8 servings

Emperor-Style Soft-Shell Crabs

24 soft-shell crabs, cleaned
1 cup cornstarch
8 eggs, beaten
vegetable oil for deep-frying
1/2 cup vegetable oil
1/4 cup chopped onion
1/4 cup chopped carrot
1/4 cup chick-peas
5 tablespoons light soy sauce
1 tablespoon mushroom soy sauce
3 tablespoons sugar
3 tablespoons white wine
1 red bell pepper, cut into slivers
chopped scallions

Coat the crabs with the cornstarch and dip into the beaten eggs. Deep-fry in vegetable oil until golden brown, about 6 minutes. Drain on paper towels.

Heat 1/2 cup vegetable oil in a sauté pan. Add the onion, carrot and chick-peas and stir-fry until tender, about 5 minutes. Stir in the soy sauces, sugar and wine.

To serve, spoon the vegetable mixture onto serving plates and top with 3 soft-shell crabs per serving. Sprinkle with the red bell pepper and chopped scallions.

Makes 8 servings

Grand Marnier Prawns

MARNIER SAUCE
1 cup mayonnaise
1/4 cup light cream
1 tablespoon fresh lemon juice
2 tablespoons Grand Marnier
1/4 cup sugar

PRAWNS
vegetable oil for deep-frying
5 pounds prawns or extra-large shrimp, peeled and deveined
4 pounds baby bok choy, cut into halves lengthwise
1 pound snow peas
2 green bell peppers, sliced
2 red bell peppers, sliced
8 ounces wood ear mushrooms
1/4 cup vegetable oil
3 tablespoons chopped garlic
3 tablespoons sugar
3 tablespoons chicken powder
salt to taste

To prepare the sauce, combine the mayonnaise, cream, lemon juice, Grand Marnier and sugar in a bowl and mix well.

To prepare the prawns, heat vegetable oil in a deep fryer. Deep-fry the prawns until cooked through, about 2 to 3 minutes. Remove to paper towels to drain.

Blanch the bok choy, snow peas, bell peppers and mushrooms in boiling water in a saucepan. Plunge into ice water to stop the cooking process.

Heat 1/4 cup vegetable oil in a wok. Add the garlic and stir-fry for 2 to 3 seconds. Add the blanched vegetables, sugar and chicken powder. Season with salt. Serve with the sauce for dipping.

Makes 8 servings

竹

Jade Sea Scallops

64 large scallops
1 pound shrimp, peeled, deveined and finely minced
1 cup cornstarch
vegetable oil for deep-frying
1/4 cup vegetable oil
1 1/2 tablespoons chopped garlic
1 1/2 ounces black beans
3 tablespoons white wine
5 cups Chicken Stock *(page 26)*
salt to taste
3 tablespoons sugar
3 tablespoons chicken powder
2 tablespoons cornstarch
1 1/2 tablespoons sesame oil
48 spears Chinese broccoli, blanched, for garnish

Cut a horizontal pocket in each scallop, taking care not to cut all the way through. Stuff the shrimp into the scallop pockets. Coat with 1 cup cornstarch. Deep-fry in heated vegetable oil just until cooked through.

Heat 1/4 cup vegetable oil in a wok and add the garlic, black beans, wine and Chicken Stock. Stir in the salt, sugar, chicken powder, 2 tablespoons cornstarch and sesame oil. Add the scallops and stir-fry until heated through. Garnish with Chinese broccoli.

Makes 8 servings

Asian Eggplant with Garlic Sauce

vegetable oil for deep-frying
5 pounds eggplant, cut into 1/4-inch slices
1 tablespoon sesame oil
1 tablespoon chopped garlic
8 pieces chile pepper
5 cups Chicken Stock *(page 26)*
3 tablespoons mushroom soy sauce
3 tablespoons light soy sauce
3 tablespoons oyster sauce
5 tablespoons sugar
1 tablespoon chicken powder
1 tablespoon white vinegar
1/2 cup hot sauce
2 tablespoons cornstarch
2 tablespoons water
1 bunch scallions, chopped

Heat vegetable oil in a deep fryer and deep-fry the eggplant until cooked through, about 5 to 8 minutes. Remove to paper towels to drain.

Heat the sesame oil in a wok. Add the garlic, chile pepper, Chicken Stock, soy sauces, oyster sauce, sugar, chicken powder, vinegar and hot sauce; mix well.

Whisk the cornstarch and water together in a cup to make a slurry. Add the slurry, scallions and fried eggplant to the wok. Stir-fry until thickened and heated through.

Makes 8 servings

Curry Fried Rice

2 tablespoons vegetable oil
12 ounces baby shrimp
2 eggs, beaten
1/4 cup chopped onion
12 ounces cooked chicken, chopped
1 tablespoon curry powder
2 pounds white rice, cooked
1 teaspoon salt
1 teaspoon chicken powder
chopped scallions for garnish

Heat the vegetable oil in a wok and stir-fry the shrimp until pink, about 3 to 4 minutes. Remove with a slotted spoon to paper towels to drain.

Reheat the vegetable oil and add the eggs and onion. Stir-fry until cooked through. Add the shrimp, chicken, curry powder, rice, salt and chicken powder; mix well. Stir-fry until heated through. Garnish with scallions.

Makes 8 servings

Just a few feet from the gaming action, you'll find The Longhouse, which is designed to represent the traditional dwelling of the Mohegans. Wooden antlers grace the ceiling and sepia photographs of early Mohegan leaders transport you to a bygone era.

Pan-Roasted Salmon with Crab Meat Stuffing
and Citrus Beurre Blanc

Blackened Tuna
Whipped Cheddar Polenta Roasted Tomato Relish

Jumbo Lump Crab Cakes
Red Pepper Rémoulade Lemon Lime Aïoli

Grilled Porterhouse with Maytag Blue Cheese Sauce
Sweet Potato Brûlée
Broccoli and Cauliflower au Gratin

Calf's Liver with Caramelized Onions and Bacon

Longhouse Crispy Chicken

Smoked Barbecued Ribs
Onion Strings

Pan-Roasted Salmon with Crab Meat Stuffing and Citrus Beurre Blanc

SALMON
8 (8-ounce) salmon fillets
Crab Mixture ***(page 130)***
1 cup (2 sticks) butter, melted
1 cup fresh lemon juice
1 cup white wine
2 leeks, cleaned and julienned, white and light green portions only
2 cups all-purpose flour
kosher salt and freshly ground black pepper to taste
vegetable oil for deep-frying

CITRUS BEURRE BLANC
2 shallots, sliced
1/2 cup white wine vinegar
1 cup white wine
1 lemon, sliced
1 teaspoon black peppercorns
1 cup heavy cream
1 cup (2 sticks) butter, cubed
juice of 1 lemon

To prepare the salmon, preheat the oven to 425 degrees. Butterfly the salmon fillets lengthwise and stuff with the Crab Mixture. Place in a baking pan. Mix the butter, lemon juice and wine in a bowl. Pour over the salmon and bake for 15 minutes.

Toss the leeks in a mixture of the flour, kosher salt and pepper. Heat the vegetable oil to 375 degrees. Deep-fry the leeks in the oil until golden brown. Remove with a slotted spoon and drain on paper towels.

To prepare the citrus beurre blanc, combine the shallots, vinegar, wine, lemon and peppercorns in a saucepan. Cook until the liquid evaporates. Add the heavy cream and cook until reduced by 2/3. Remove from the heat and slowly whisk in the butter. Stir in the lemon juice; strain.

To serve, spoon the beurre blanc into the center of each serving plate; place the salmon in the sauce and top with fried leeks.

Makes 8 servings

Blackened Tuna

2 cups (4 sticks) butter
4 ounces blackening spice
8 (8-ounce) tuna steaks
Whipped Cheddar Polenta ***(below)***
Roasted Tomato Relish ***(page 129)***

Melt the butter in a saucepan and stir in the blackening spice. Heat a cast-iron skillet until it starts to smoke. Dip the tuna steaks into the butter and place in the skillet. Sear on both sides until done to taste.

To serve, spoon the Whipped Cheddar Polenta onto the center of each serving plate. Place the tuna on the polenta and top with the Roasted Tomato Relish.

Makes 8 servings

Whipped Cheddar Polenta

2 shallots, chopped
1/2 cup (1 stick) butter
4 cups Chicken Stock ***(page 26)***
4 cups heavy cream
1 bay leaf
4 cups uncooked instant yellow polenta
2 cups (8 ounces) shredded aged sharp Cheddar cheese
1 tablespoon Worcestershire sauce
kosher salt and freshly ground black pepper to taste

Sauté the shallots in the butter in a saucepan until tender. Add the Chicken Stock, cream and bay leaf and bring to a simmer. Whisk in the polenta gradually and simmer for 30 minutes or until the polenta is no longer grainy. Discard the bay leaf.

Whisk in the cheese and Worcestershire sauce and season with kosher salt and pepper. Add additional hot cream if necessary for the desired consistency.

Makes 8 servings

Roasted Tomato Relish

1 pint yellow cherry tomatoes
1 pint red cherry tomatoes
1 tablespoon extra-virgin olive oil
kosher salt and freshly ground black pepper to taste
1/4 cup extra-virgin olive oil
2 tablespoons fresh basil chiffonade
1 cup marinated cippolini onions, cut into halves

Cut the cherry tomatoes into halves and toss with 1 tablespoon olive oil in a bowl. Season with kosher salt and pepper.

Preheat the oven to 250 degrees. Place the tomatoes on a roasting rack in a baking pan. Bake for 2 hours. Cool to room temperature.

Whisk 1/4 cup olive oil, basil, kosher salt and pepper together in a large bowl. Fold in the onions and roasted tomatoes gradually.

Makes 8 servings

Jumbo Lump Crab Cakes

CRAB MIXTURE
2 cups mayonnaise
4 eggs, beaten
1 teaspoon Dijon mustard
1 teaspoon Worcestershire sauce
1 teaspoon Old Bay seasoning
1 tablespoon chopped fresh parsley
juice of 1 lemon
2 to 3 cups fresh bread crumbs
2 (16-ounce) cans jumbo lump crab meat

CRAB CAKE ASSEMBLY
canola oil or vegetable oil for deep-frying
6 egg roll wrappers
Red Pepper Rémoulade ***(below)***
Lemon-Lime Aïoli ***(page 131)***

To prepare the crab mixture, whisk the mayonnaise, eggs, Dijon mustard, Worcestershire sauce, Old Bay seasoning, parsley and lemon juice together in a large bowl. Add enough bread crumbs to bind the mixture. Fold in the crab meat gradually, taking care not to break up the lumps. Scoop with a 2-ounce scoop and shape into cakes. Prepare and chill for up to 1 day if desired.

To assemble the crab cakes, heat the canola oil to 375 degrees in a deep fryer and deep-fry the crab cakes until golden brown. Remove from the fryer and drain on paper towels. Slice the egg roll wrappers into thin strips. Deep-fry in the heated oil until golden brown, about 30 to 60 seconds. Drain on paper towels.

To serve, place each crab cake on a small round plate. Top with the egg roll strips and drizzle 1 tablespoon each Red Pepper Rémoulade and Lemon-Lime Aïoli around the plate.

Makes 8 servings

Red Pepper Rémoulade

1/4 cup roasted red peppers
1 tablespoon chopped fresh cilantro
1 teaspoon brown mustard
1 cup mayonnaise

Combine the roasted red peppers, cilantro, brown mustard and mayonnaise in a food processor or blender and process until smooth.

Makes 8 servings

Lemon-Lime Aïoli

1 cup mayonnaise
1/2 teaspoon grated lemon zest
1/2 teaspoon grated lime zest
juice of 1 lemon
1 teaspoon Dijon mustard

Combine the mayonnaise, lemon zest, lime zest, lemon juice and Dijon mustard in a small bowl and mix until smooth.

Makes 8 servings

Grilled Porterhouse with Maytag Blue Cheese Sauce

MAYTAG BLUE CHEESE SAUCE
2 cloves garlic, chopped
1 teaspoon olive oil
1/2 cup white wine
2 cups heavy cream
1 cup (4 ounces) crumbled Maytag blue cheese

STEAKS
8 (22-ounce) prime porterhouse steaks
1 cup Montreal steak seasoning
Sweet Potato Brûlée *(below)*
Broccoli and Cauliflower au Gratin *(page 133)*

To prepare the cheese sauce, sauté the garlic in the olive oil in a sauté pan until tender, taking care not to burn. Deglaze the pan with the wine and cook until reduced by 1/2. Add the heavy cream and cook until reduced by 1/3. Stir in the blue cheese. Keep warm.

To prepare the steaks, heat a charcoal grill. Season the steaks on both sides with the steak seasoning and place on the grill. Grill for 3 minutes, then turn 45 degrees in the opposite direction in order to create a diamond pattern and grill for 3 minutes longer. Turn the steaks and grill in the same manner, cooking each turn for 3 minutes for rare or until done to taste.

Serve with the blue cheese sauce, Sweet Potato Brûlée and Broccoli and Cauliflower au Gratin.

Makes 8 servings

Sweet Potato Brûlée

8 sweet potatoes
1/2 cup heavy cream
1 egg
2 tablespoons brown sugar
1 tablespoon vanilla extract
1 teaspoon ground cinnamon
1 teaspoon nutmeg
1/2 cup Sugar in the Raw®

Preheat the oven to 350 degrees. Roast the sweet potatoes for 40 minutes or until tender. Cool, peel and place through a food mill or ricer. Reduce the oven temperature to 300 degrees. Whisk the cream, egg, brown sugar, vanilla, cinnamon and nutmeg together in a bowl. Fold in the sweet potatoes. Spoon into 8 scalloped brûlée dishes or ramekins, filling to the rim and leveling off.

Bake for 10 to 15 minutes. Remove from oven and sprinkle with the sugar, shaking off the excess. Broil until the sugar is melted and bubbly, about 2 minutes.

Makes 8 servings

Broccoli and Cauliflower au Gratin

salt to taste
4 cups broccoli florets
4 cups cauliflower florets
6 cloves garlic, chopped
1 tablespoon olive oil
4 cups heavy cream
kosher salt and pepper to taste
3 cups (12 ounces) grated
Parmesan cheese
1 cup panko (Asian bread crumbs)
2 tablespoons chopped fresh parsley
3 tablespoons butter, melted

Bring a large saucepan of salted water to a boil and add the broccoli and cauliflower. Cook until tender, about 5 minutes. Drain and place in ice water to stop the cooking process, drain and reserve.

Sauté the garlic in the olive oil until tender, taking care not to burn. Add the heavy cream and bring just to a simmer. Season with kosher salt and pepper and whisk in the cheese. Pour over the broccoli and cauliflower and mix well. Spoon into 8 ramekins.

Preheat the oven to 325 degrees. Mix the bread crumbs, parsley and butter together in a bowl. Sprinkle over the vegetable mixture. Bake until hot and golden brown, about 10 minutes.

Makes 8 servings

Calf's Liver with Caramelized Onions and Bacon

2 tablespoons butter
2 Spanish onions, sliced
1 tablespoon fresh thyme leaves
kosher salt and freshly ground black pepper to taste
16 slices bacon
2 cups all-purpose flour
1/2 cup olive oil
2 tablespoons butter
8 (6-ounce) slices calf's liver
1/2 cup Demi Glace ***(page 101)***

Melt 2 tablespoons butter in a sauté pan and add the onions. Cook until the onions begin to caramelize without stirring. Toss the onions and cook until caramelized on all sides. Sprinkle with the thyme leaves and season with kosher salt and pepper.

Preheat the oven to 400 degrees. Arrange the bacon on a baking sheet and bake until crisp; drain on paper towels.

Reduce the oven temperature to 375 degrees. Season the flour with kosher salt and pepper to taste. Heat an ovenproof sauté pan over medium-high heat and add the olive oil and 2 tablespoons butter. Coat the liver slices with the flour mixture, shaking off the excess. Sauté in the olive oil and butter until golden brown on both sides. Bake in the oven until done to taste.

To serve, transfer the liver to serving plates. Top with the caramelized onions and bacon; drizzle with the Demi Glace.

Makes 8 servings

Longhouse Crispy Chicken

Garlic Cheese Butter
1 pound (4 sticks) unsalted butter, cubed
4 cloves garlic, chopped
2 tablespoons chopped fresh parsley
2 tablespoons shredded Monterey Jack cheese
2 tablespoons shredded Cheddar cheese

Chicken
8 chicken breasts
1 pound Swiss cheese, sliced
1 pound smoked ham, sliced
12 cups all-purpose flour
kosher salt and freshly ground black pepper to taste
12 eggs, beaten
12 cups panko (see Note)
vegetable oil for deep-frying

To prepare the garlic cheese butter, whip the butter in a large mixing bowl fitted with a paddle until smooth. Add the garlic, parsley, Monterey Jack cheese and Cheddar cheese gradually, mixing constantly until smooth. Chill until serving time.

To prepare the chicken, place the chicken breasts skin side down 3 inches apart on a work surface. Cover with plastic wrap and pound lightly with a mallet until even, taking care not to tear.

Place 2 slices of Swiss cheese and 2 slices of ham in the center of each chicken breast and place 1 tablespoon of garlic cheese butter over the ham. Roll lengthwise to enclose the filling.

Mix the flour with kosher salt and pepper in a shallow bowl or pan. Place the eggs in a second bowl. Place the bread crumbs in a third bowl. Coat each chicken roll with the flour, shaking off the excess. Dip into the egg and then roll in the crumbs. Place on a tray and refrigerate for 2 hours or overnight.

Preheat the oven to 375 degrees. Heat the vegetable oil to 350 degrees in a deep fryer. Add the chicken rolls and deep-fry until golden brown, about 8 to 10 minutes. Remove to a baking pan and bake for 15 minutes or until the internal temperature reaches 165 degrees. Let stand for 5 minutes before serving.

NOTE: Panko bread crumbs are available at Asian markets or in the Asian section of your supermarket.

Makes 8 servings

Smoked Barbecued Ribs

Peach Barbecue Sauce
1 red onion, chopped
1 tablespoon vegetable oil
1 cup chopped peaches in syrup
4 quarts barbecue sauce

Spice Rub
2 tablespoons paprika
1 tablespoon ground ancho chile
1 tablespoon chipotle powder
2 tablespoons brown sugar
1 tablespoon sugar
1 teaspoon granulated garlic
1 tablespoon onion powder
2 tablespoons kosher salt
1 tablespoon freshly ground black pepper
1 tablespoon ground cumin

Ribs
4 racks baby back ribs or St. Louis ribs
Onion Strings ***(page 137)***
Pommerey Mustard Sauce ***(page 137)***

To prepare the barbecue sauce, sauté the onions in the vegetable oil in a saucepan until translucent. Add the peaches and barbecue sauce. Simmer for 10 minutes. Process in a food processor or blender until smooth. Store in the refrigerator.

To prepare the Spice Rub, combine the paprika, ancho chile, chipotle powder, brown sugar, sugar, garlic, onion powder, kosher salt, pepper and cumin in a bowl and mix well.

To prepare the ribs, sprinkle both sides with the spice rub. Marinate in the refrigerator overnight.

Smoke or roast the ribs at 220 degrees for 2 1/2 hours. Let the ribs cool and cut into serving pieces between the bones. Grill the ribs until done to taste, basting frequently with the barbecue sauce.

To serve, top the ribs with the Onion Strings and drizzle with the Pommerey Mustard Sauce.

Makes 8 servings

Onion Strings

2 onions, very thinly sliced
1 cup milk
4 cups all-purpose flour
kosher salt and freshly ground black pepper to taste
vegetable oil for deep-frying

Soak the onions in the milk in a bowl; drain. Toss in a mixture of the flour, kosher salt and pepper, coating well and shaking off the excess. Deep-fry the onion strings in vegetable oil heated to 375 degrees. Remove with a slotted spoon and drain on paper towels.

Makes 8 servings

Pommerey Mustard Sauce

1 cup mayonnaise
1 tablespoon Pommerey mustard
2 tablespoons heavy cream
1/4 cup sour cream

Combine the mayonnaise, mustard, heavy cream and sour cream in a food processor or blender. Process until smooth.

Makes 8 servings

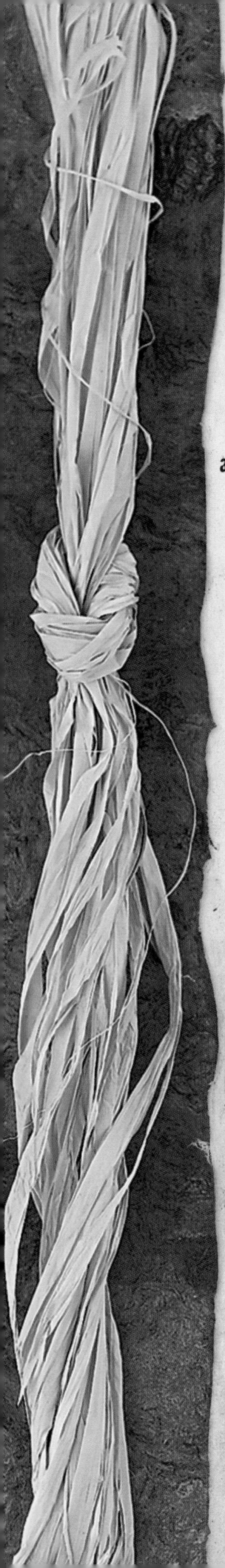

Mohegans, past and present, shared the universal human weakness for things sweet. Traditionally, Mohegans enjoyed the sweetness of wild berries and grapes, both fresh and dried. They also used them, along with maple sugar and birch sugar, to sweeten foods. The Mohegan Sun pastry chefs today concoct much more tempting desserts and sweets to tease the tastes of visitors; they can be found in every food venue at Mohegan Sun.

The Wedding Cake

Carrot Cake

Falling Chocolate Cake with Raspberry Sauce

White Chocolate Mousse

Chocolate Blackout

Fruit-Topped New York Cheesecakes

Classic Crème Brûlée

Warm Apple Cobbler with Streusel Topping

Tiramisù

Wihksapākat

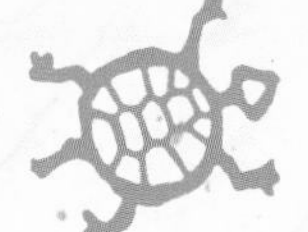

The Wedding Cake

Mohegan Sun unveiled the world's largest wedding cake at the New England Bridal Showcase held in the Uncas Ballroom on February 8, 2004. The seven-tiered, 15,032-pound, eighteen-foot wedding cake shattered the world record for the largest wedding cake in the *Guinness Book of World Records.* It was almost three times the weight of the cake that formerly held the title, baked at Universal Studios in Florida.

The vanilla-flavored cake was decorated with chocolate bows and hearts. It had a frosting flavored with vanilla and almond. The cake used 10,000 pounds of cake batter and 4,810 pounds of creamy frosting. When complete, it weighed more than five Volkswagen Beetles and could serve up to 59,000 people.

To create the cake, a team of fifty-seven chefs and pastry artisans baked seven hundred 18×24-inch vanilla sheet cakes. Then, using frosting to stick them together, they created two hundred five- and six-layer bricks, which were put together to form the tiers of the cake. Steel discs were used as separators for the tiers, and two fork lifts helped raise each tier as the wedding cake took shape.

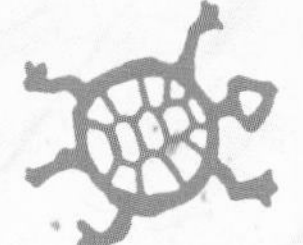

Carrot Cake

3 cups sugar
2 1/2 cups vegetable oil
7 large eggs
4 cups all-purpose flour
1 tablespoon ground cinnamon
2 teaspoons baking soda
2 teaspoons vanilla extract
1 teaspoon salt
1/2 teaspoon ground nutmeg
5 1/2 cups shredded carrots
1 1/4 cups crushed pineapple
1 1/4 cups flaked coconut
6 ounces coconut, toasted
Cream Cheese Frosting *(below)*
Carrot Garnish *(page 143)*

Preheat the oven to 350 degrees. Combine the sugar, vegetable oil and eggs in a mixing bowl and beat for 1 minute. Add the flour, cinnamon, baking soda, vanilla extract, salt and nutmeg and beat at high speed for 2 minutes. Fold in the carrots, pineapple and flaked coconut.

Coat two 10-inch cake pans evenly with nonstick cooking spray. Spoon the batter into the pans. Bake for 20 to 25 minutes or until firm. Remove from the pans and cool completely on a rack before frosting.

Spread the Cream Cheese Frosting over the top of 1 cake. Slice the second cake into halves horizontally and place 1/2 on top of the frosted cake; frost the top. Top with the remaining 1/2 cake. Spread the top and side of the cake with the remaining frosting. Press the toasted coconut all around the side of the cake.

Pipe 12 rosettes around the top of the cake with the frosting reserved from the Carrot Garnish. Arrange 1 carrot on each rosette.

Makes 12 servings

Cream Cheese Frosting

1 cup (2 sticks) butter, softened
1 cup shortening
32 ounces cream cheese, softened
1 tablespoon lemon juice
1 teaspoon vanilla extract
32 ounces confectioners' sugar

Cream the butter and shortening in a mixing bowl until smooth. Add the cream cheese and mix until smooth. Blend in the lemon juice and vanilla extract. Add the confectioners' sugar and mix until smooth.

Frosts 1 cake

Carrot Garnish

1/4 cup (1/2 stick) butter
1/4 cup shortening
8 ounces cream cheese, softened
1 drop of lemon juice
1 drop of vanilla extract
8 ounces confectioners' sugar
orange food coloring
green food coloring

Cream the butter and shortening in a mixing bowl until smooth. Add the cream cheese and mix until smooth. Blend in the lemon juice and vanilla extract. Add the confectioners' sugar and mix until smooth.

Add a few drops of orange food coloring to 3 ounces of the frosting. Spoon into a pastry bag and pipe 12 carrot sticks onto parchment paper. Add a few drops of green food coloring to 2 ounces of the frosting. Spoon into a clean pastry bag and top each carrot stick with a green top. Freeze until hardened. Spoon the remaining frosting into a clean pastry bag and reserve.

Makes 12 carrots and rosettes

Falling Chocolate Cake with Raspberry Sauce

Raspberry Sauce
4 cups fresh or frozen raspberries
1/2 cup white sugar
1 to 3 teaspoons fresh lemon juice

Chocolate Cake
2 tablespoons unsalted butter
2 tablespoons all-purpose flour
12 ounces bittersweet chocolate, coarsely chopped
1 cup (2 sticks) unsalted butter
1 cup white sugar
1/2 cup all-purpose flour
6 large eggs
4 cups vanilla ice cream, for serving
2 tablespoons powdered sugar, for garnish
6 fresh mint sprigs, for garnish

To make the raspberry sauce: Place the raspberries and sugar in a small saucepan and bring to a boil, stirring, over high heat. Boil until the sugar dissolves. Add lemon juice to taste. Let cool.

Place half the sauce in a food processor fitted with a steel blade and purée. Combine with the remaining sauce, cover, and refrigerate until cold.

Preheat the oven to 350 degrees. Generously butter and flour six 8-ounce ramekins.

Place the chocolate and butter in the top of a double boiler over simmering water. Stir until completely melted. Set aside to cool.

Place the sugar, flour and eggs in a large bowl and beat until thick and fluffy, about 5 minutes. Gently beat in the cooled chocolate mixture.

Pour the batter into the prepared ramekins, filling them two-thirds to three-quarters of the way up the sides. Bake until they begin to puff up, about 15 minutes. Run a knife around the edge of each ramekin and turn the ramekin upside down on plates to unmold.

Serve each warm cake surround by sauce, with a scoop of vanilla ice cream alongside. Garnish with the powdered sugar and sprigs of fresh mint.

Serves 6

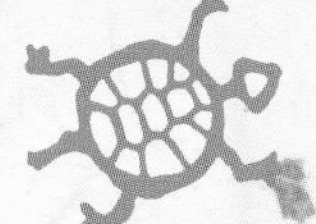

White Chocolate Mousse

9 ounces good-quality white chocolate, such as Lindt
3/4 teaspoon unflavored gelatin
1 tablespoon water
1 ounce Cointreau liqueur
3 large egg yolks
3 tablespoons sugar
3 large egg whites
2 teaspoons sugar
10 ounces heavy cream
fresh berries for garnish

Melt the white chocolate in a double boiler over simmering water. Let stand over warm water.

Sprinkle the gelatin over the water in a bowl. Let stand until the gelatin absorbs the water, about 4 minutes. Heat the Cointreau in a saucepan and add the gelatin. Stir until the gelatin dissolves completely.

Whip the egg yolks with 3 tablespoons sugar in a mixing bowl until thick and pale yellow. Stir in the chocolate; the mixture will tighten up. Add the warm Cointreau mixture immediately and stir until smooth.

Whip the egg whites with 2 teaspoons sugar in a mixing bowl until soft peaks form. Fold into the chocolate mixture.

Whip the cream in a mixing bowl until soft peaks form. Fold into the chocolate mixture. Spoon into 3-ounce molds or ramekins. Chill for 8 hours or longer.

To serve, unmold the mousse onto serving plates and garnish with fresh berries.

Makes 8 servings

Chocolate Blackout

1 1/4 cups heavy cream
10 ounces bittersweet chocolate, finely chopped
2 eggs, beaten
1 (9-inch) chocolate cookie crust
Chocolate Ganache *(below)*
Chocolate Mousse *(page 147)*
2 cups heavy cream
1 cup chocolate cookie crumbs
1 pint raspberries

Preheat the oven to 325 degrees. Heat 1 1/4 cups cream in a saucepan until bubbles form at the edge. Remove from the heat and add the chopped chocolate. Let stand for 3 minutes, then stir until melted. Stir in the eggs.

Pour into the cookie crust and bake for 15 minutes or until the edge is firm but the center is wobbly. Spread 8 ounces of the Chocolate Ganache over the baked layer. Spread the Chocolate Mousse over the ganache layer. Place in the freezer just until the mousse is set; do not freeze.

Combine 2 ounces of the Chocolate Ganache and 2 cups cream in a mixing bowl and whip until firm peaks form. Spread over the Chocolate Mousse, mounding in the center. Press the cookie crumbs onto the mousse layer.

Purée the raspberries in a food processor and strain through a fine mesh sieve. Drizzle the raspberry sauce around the plates to serve.

Makes 6 to 8 servings

Chocolate Ganache

3/4 cup heavy cream
10 ounces bittersweet chocolate, finely chopped

Heat the cream in a saucepan until bubbles form at the edge. Pour the warm cream over the chocolate in a bowl. Let stand for 10 minutes. Stir until smooth.

Makes 16 ounces

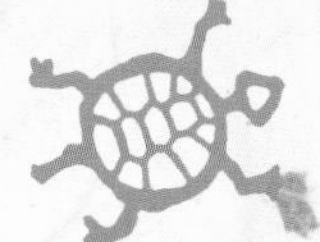

Chocolate Mousse

6 ounces bittersweet chocolate, finely chopped
3 tablespoons butter
1 teaspoon vanilla extract
1 1/2 teaspoons unflavored gelatin
3 tablespoons water
3 large egg yolks
3 tablespoons sugar
1/2 cup heavy cream
3 large egg whites
1/4 cup sugar

Melt the chocolate with the butter and vanilla extract in a double boiler. Set aside. Sprinkle the gelatin over the water in a bowl and let stand for 5 minutes to soften.

Combine the egg yolks, gelatin and 3 tablespoons sugar in a metal bowl and place over boiling water. Cook until thick and pale yellow, about 6 to 8 minutes, whisking constantly. Remove from the heat and whisk into the melted chocolate.

Beat the cream in a mixing bowl until soft peaks form. Fold into the chocolate mixture. Beat the egg whites in a mixing bowl until soft peaks form. Add 1/4 cup sugar gradually, increasing the speed to high and continuing to beat until stiff peaks form. Stir 1/3 of the beaten egg white mixture into the chocolate mixture. Fold in the remaining egg white mixture. Chill in the refrigerator.

Makes 6 to 8 servings

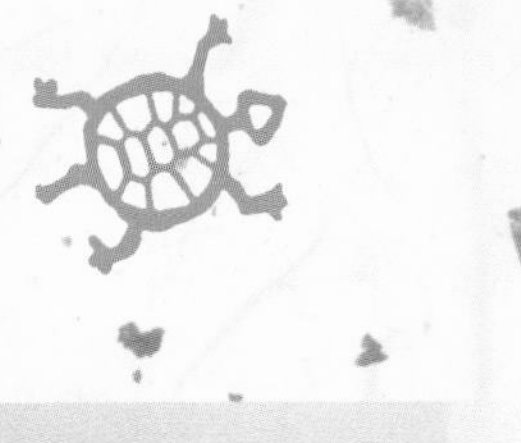

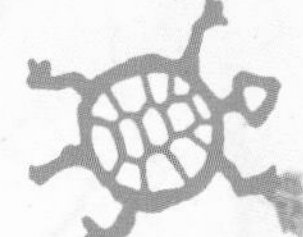

Fruit-Topped New York Cheesecakes

CHEESECAKES
1/4 cup fine graham cracker crumbs
26 ounces cream cheese, softened
1 cup confectioners' sugar
1/4 cup cornstarch
3 large eggs
3 tablespoons heavy cream
1 tablespoon fresh lemon juice
1 tablespoon vanilla extract

CHEESECAKE TOPPING
1 pint (2 cups) heavy cream
1/4 cup confectioners' sugar
1 teaspoon vanilla extract
seasonal fruits and berries

APRICOT GLAZE
4 ounces apricot jam
2 tablespoons water

To prepare the cheesecakes, preheat the oven to 325 degrees. Spray six 3 1/2-inch ramekins with nonstick cooking spray. Dust the ramekins with the graham cracker crumbs. Set aside.

Blend the cream cheese, confectioners' sugar and cornstarch in a small mixing bowl until smooth. Add the eggs 1 at a time, mixing well after each addition and scraping the bowl. Add the cream, lemon juice and vanilla extract and mix until smooth.

Pour the batter evenly into the ramekins and place in a 9×13-inch baking pan. Fill the pan with water halfway up the sides of the ramekins. Bake for 2 hours or until firm. Chill in the refrigerator for 4 hours or longer. Tap the ramekins on the sides to loosen the cheesecakes and invert onto serving plates.

To prepare the topping, combine the cream, confectioners' sugar and vanilla extract in a mixing bowl. Whip with a whisk until soft peaks form. Spoon the whipped cream into a pastry bag and pipe large rosettes on top of each cheesecake. Top with seasonal fruits and berries.

To prepare the glaze, combine the apricot jam and water in a small saucepan and cook over low heat just until heated through. Brush over the fruits and berries.

Makes 6 servings

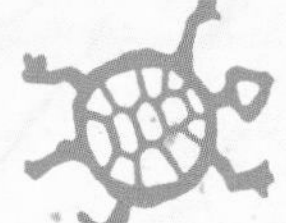

Classic Crème Brûlée

4 cups heavy cream
1 whole vanilla bean
1/2 cup sugar
7 large egg yolks
1/2 teaspoon salt
3 tablespoons brown sugar
fresh berries for garnish

Preheat the oven to 300 degrees. Add the cream to a small saucepan. Split the vanilla bean in 1/2 and scrape the seeds into the cream. Add the vanilla bean to the cream. Heat gently until hot. Strain through a fine mesh sieve and discard the solids.

Whisk the sugar, egg yolks and salt together in a small bowl. Add 1/3 of the hot cream mixture to the egg yolk mixture, stirring to temper the eggs so that they do not scramble. Stir the egg yolk mixture into the hot cream mixture.

Fill ceramic soufflé dishes or ramekins 3/4 full and place in a larger pan with a water bath. Bake for approximately 1 hour or until firm; cool.

Top with the brown sugar at serving time. Broil until bubbly, crystallized and golden brown. You may also use a kitchen torch according to the directions, watching carefully to avoid burning. Garnish with fresh berries.

Makes 6 servings

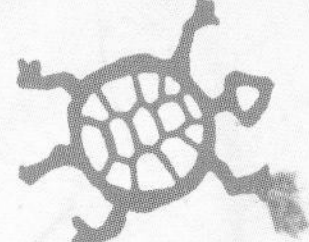

Warm Apple Cobbler with Streusel Topping

Streusel Topping
1/4 cup all-purpose flour
1/4 cup sugar
1/2 cup packed brown sugar
1/3 cup raw almonds, sliced
1/2 cup (1 stick) butter, cubed
1/4 cup rolled oats

Cobbler
6 Granny Smith apples
1/3 cup brown sugar
3 ounces maple syrup
pinch of ground cinnamon
pinch of nutmeg
1 tablespoon Apple Jack brandy
1/2 cup raisins
vanilla ice cream or frozen yogurt

To prepare the topping, combine the flour, sugar, brown sugar and almonds in a small bowl. Cut in the butter until crumbly. Add the oats and mix well.

To prepare the cobbler, preheat the oven to 350 degrees. Peel and core the apples and cut into quarters. Place in a small saucepan.Add the brown sugar, maple syrup, cinnamon, nutmeg and brandy. Cook over medium heat for 5 minutes, stirring constantly. Add the raisins and cook for 1 minute longer.

Fill 6 ramekins 3/4 full. Top with the Streusel Topping. Bake until golden brown, about 35 minutes. Serve warm with vanilla ice cream or frozen yogurt.

Makes 6 servings

Tiramisù

3 large egg yolks
1/4 cup sugar
1/3 cup Kahlúa
8 ounces mascarpone cheese, at room temperature
1/2 cup heavy cream
2 large egg whites
1 teaspoon sugar
2/3 cup Kahlúa
1/4 cup rum
1/4 cup espresso
2 packages ladyfingers
baking cocoa for dusting
whipped cream, fresh berries, fresh mint sprigs, chocolate sauce and/or Chocolate Sticks (see Note) for garnish

Beat the egg yolks with 1/4 cup sugar in a double boiler until light in color. Add 1/3 cup Kahlúa and cook over gently simmering water until the mixture begins to thicken, whisking constantly. Remove from the heat and fold in the mascarpone cheese.

Beat the cream in a mixing bowl until soft peaks form. Fold into the mascarpone mixture. Beat the egg whites with 1 teaspoon sugar in a mixing bowl until soft peaks form. Fold into the mascarpone mixture.

Combine 2/3 cup Kahlúa, the rum and espresso in a shallow dish. Dip the ladyfingers into the mixture and arrange several in a single layer in the bottom of a 9x13-inch glass dish or 9-inch bowl. Spread with 1/3 of the mascarpone mixture. Continue to layer the ladyfingers and mascarpone mixture in the dish until all the ingredients are used and finishing with a layer of the mascarpone mixture. Dust with baking cocoa and refrigerate for 4 hours or longer.

Cut or scoop the tiramisù into individual servings. Garnish with whipped cream, fresh berries, mint, chocolate sauce and/or Chocolate Sticks.

NOTE: To make Chocolate Sticks, melt 2 ounces of good–quality chocolate in a double boiler over simmering water. Spoon into a pastry bag and pipe thin sticks onto parchment paper. Chill in the refrigerator until firm.

Makes 6 servings

Index

T

For additional copies of this cookbook, contact:
The Cookbook Marketplace
2451 Atrium Way
Nashville, Tennessee 37214
Telephone: 1-800-269-6839
Fax: 1-615-391-2815
www.frpbooks.com

Tribal soups and chowders are produced commercially
in four-pound pouches that serve eight to ten.
They are available at Mohegan Sun or you may order directly from:
Blount Seafood
Warren, Rhode Island
1-800-274-2526